MIKROTIK SECURITY GUIDE

MikroTik® Security Guide
Second Edition

Tyler Hart
Manito Networks, LLC

Copyright © 2017 by Manito Networks, LLC. All rights reserved.

No part of this publication may be reproduced or utilized in any form or by any means, electronic or mechanical, including photocopying, recording, or by any information storage and retrieval system, except as permitted by the United States Copyright Act, without permission in writing from the publisher.

Author: Tyler Hart

ISBN: 9781549893407

Original cover art by Martin Grandjean [CC BY-SA 3.0 (https://creativecommons.org/licenses/by-sa/3.0)], via Wikimedia Commons

The author(s) and publisher(s) make no warranties or representations with respect to the wholeness, completeness, or accuracy of the contents of this work. The author(s) and publisher(s) disclaim all warranties including any warranties of fitness for a particular purpose. Every network and information system is different, and you should consult with a professional before implementing the solutions or suggestions in this publication.

Vendor and product names are displayed in caps or initial caps, and every effort made to respect trademarks where Manito Networks, LLC is aware a trademark is claimed. Usage of trademarked product or vendor names does not constitute an endorsement of or by the trademark owner. Manito Networks, LLC is not affiliated with any vendor or product mentioned in this publication. For more information on copyrights and trademarks in this document see the online resources at https://www.manitonetworks.com.

"MikroTik" is a registered trademark of Mikrotikls, AKA MikroTik LLC.

"CCNA" and "Cisco" are registered trademarks of Cisco Technology, Inc.

"Apple" and "iOS" are registered trademarks of Apple Inc.

"Android" and "Google" are registered trademarks of Google, Inc.

"Microsoft", "Windows", and "Windows Server" are registered trademarks of Microsoft Corporation.

"FileZilla" is a registered trademarks of Tim Kosse.

All other trademarks are the property of their respective owners.

Any IP addresses and DNS names used in this guide are strictly for demonstration purposes. Some public services currently available as of this writing are referenced, and you should research the viability of those service before deciding on their use in your own networks.

For more information on Manito Networks, LLC books, online publications, and articles visit our website at the following URL:

```
https://www.manitonetworks.com
```

Contents

1 Physical Security — 1
    Securing Router Interfaces 1
    Loop Protection 4
    LCD Touchscreen 4
    Console Port 6
    Physical Device Security 7

2 Software & Services — 9
    Securing Software 10
    Securing Services 11
    Network Scan with Nmap 12
    Network Discovery Scan 13
    Securing IP Services 17
    DNS 21
    Neighbor Discovery 22
    IPv6 Neighbor Discovery 24
    MAC Services 25
    Bandwidth Test Server 26
    Remediation Scan 28
    Securing SSH 28
    API Controls 32
    FTP Controls 32
    Winbox 33
    SNMP Configuration 33
    Universal Plug and Play 36
    SOCKS Proxy 37
    Dynamic DNS Service 37

3 Segmentation with VLANs — 39
    VLAN Design 39
    Creating VLANs 41
    Addressing VLAN Interfaces 41
    Switch VLAN Configuration 42
    Firewalling VLANs 42

4 Firewalls 45
Best Practices 45
Firewall Components 46
Firewall Chains 47
Firewall Rules 49
Default Firewall Rules 51
Connection Tracking 54
Comments 56
Firewall Actions 57
Address Lists 62

5 User Credentials 65
Default Admin Account 65
Additional Accounts 65
Adverse Accounts 66
Groups 67

6 Centralizing AAA with RADIUS 71
Authentication 71
Authorization 72
Accounting and Accountability 72
Onboarding 73
Passwords 73
Offboarding 73
RADIUS and FreeRADIUS 74
FreeRADIUS Installation 74
Dictionary Files 75
FreeRADIUS Logging 78
Configuration Files 78
Windows Server 2016 RADIUS 81
RouterOS Configuration 86
RADIUS Best Practices 88

7 Wireless 89
Encryption 89
WPS 90
Security Profiles 91
Access Lists 93
Client Isolation 95

8 Best Practices 97
Run Current Stable Software 97
Run Current Firmware 98
Reverse Path Filtering (Forwarding) 99
Login Banner 99

NTP Clock Synchronization 100
Dude Syslog Event Logging 100
Dude SNMP Monitoring 102
SMB Shares 106
Backups 107
Wiping Devices 108

List of Figures

1	Winbox Safe Mode	xi
2	Winbox Safe Mode Engaged	xi
3	Winbox Quit Warning	xii
4	Command Line Safe Mode	xiii
5	Safe Mode Undo Changes	xiii
1.1	Listing Interfaces	2
1.2	Disabled Interfaces	3
1.3	Console Ports	6
2.1	List Packages	10
2.2	Disabling RouterOS Package	11
2.3	Zenmap Open	13
2.4	Microsoft Windows Nmap Scan	14
2.5	Completed Nmap Scan	15
2.6	Discovered Open Ports	15
2.7	Service Scan Results	16
2.8	Zenmap Services View	17
2.9	IP Services	18
2.10	Disabled IP Services	19
2.11	Management Subnet for Services	20
2.12	Default DNS Configuration	21
2.13	DNS Recursion Enabled	21
2.14	Default Static DNS Entry	21
2.15	Neighbor Discovery Information	22
2.16	Default Neighbor Discovery Configuration	23
2.17	Interfaces Running Neighbor Discovery	23
2.18	Disabled Neighbor Discovery Interfaces	24
2.19	MAC-Server Defaults	25
2.20	Bandwidth Test 100% CPU	26
2.21	Bandwidth Test Server Authentication	27
2.22	RoMON Service Running	28
2.23	List SSH Settings	29
2.24	Weak SSH Crypto	29
2.25	Strong SSH Crypto	30

2.26 Regenerating SSH Keys 30
2.27 PuTTY Security Alert 31
2.28 Insecure FTP Server 32
2.29 Winbox New SNMP Community 34
2.30 Cannot Remove Default Community 35
2.31 Typical SNMP Information 36
2.32 UPnP Default Configuration 36
2.33 Default SOCKS Proxy Status 37

3.1 Typical Virtual Local Area Network (LAN) (VLAN) Topology 40

4.1 Routing Packet Flow 46
4.2 Input Chain Traffic 47
4.3 Forward Chain Traffic 48
4.4 Output Chain Traffic 49
4.5 Forward Chain Rule Order 51
4.6 Default Input Chain Rules 52
4.7 Default Forward Chain Rules 53
4.8 Default Output Chain Rules 54
4.9 Invalid Connections 56
4.10 Secure Shell (SSH) Firewall Log 60
4.11 Logged ICMP Traffic 60
4.12 ICMP Reject Results 61
4.13 ICMP Drop Results 62
4.14 Address Group Topology 63

5.1 Printing Active Users 69
5.2 User Logged In Entries 69

6.1 FreeRADIUS Service Status 74
6.2 FreeRADIUS Log 75
6.3 FreeRADIUS Dictionary Files 76
6.4 MikroTik Dictionary File Attributes 77
6.5 Network Policy Server (NPS) Manager Window 82
6.6 Register NPS with Active Directory 83
6.7 RouterOS RADIUS Host 87
6.8 Terminal RADIUS Status 87

7.1 New Wireless Security Profile 91
7.2 Selecting a Wireless Security Profile 92
7.3 Wireless Access List 94

8.1 RouterBoard Version 98
8.2 Displaying Login Banner 100
8.3 Dude Syslog Settings 101
8.4 Dude Syslog Events 102

8.5	Dude Default SNMP Profiles	102
8.6	Dude New SNMP Profile	103
8.7	Dude SNMP Profile in Winbox	104
8.8	Winbox SNMP Trap Configuration	105
8.9	Default SMB Settings	106
8.10	SMB Guest User	107
8.11	Resetting Device Configuration	108
8.12	Winbox Reset Configuration	108

Preface

This book was written to help you configure MikroTik RouterBoard devices securely for your organization or home. While the MikroTik Router Hardening article I wrote gets more than a thousand visitors each week there's only so much that can fit comfortably in a blog post. This book is an opportunity for us to explore MikroTik security more in-depth and implement best practices in your environment. Hopefully the recommendations presented here become part of your security culture, and I hope you discover something new about MikroTik in the process.

What This Book Is

This book is an on-the-job reference for implementing and operating MikroTik RouterOS devices securely. The intended audience is network administrators and technicians responsible for installing and configuring RouterOS devices. It is also intended for IT decision makers responsible for the security of their networks or those of their customers. Commands and design guidelines in this book can also be the starting point of RouterOS configuration templates to make secure device provisioning an easy, repeatable process.

What This Book Is Not

This book is not an introduction to basic networking, subnetting, or RouterOS fundamentals. You should already be familiar with the following tools and concepts before attempting to secure MikroTik networks:

- Basic RouterOS console usage
- The MikroTik Winbox interface
- Network fundamentals including TCP/IP ports and protocols
- Troubleshooting and configuration tools like *ping*, *traceroute*, *telnet*, *ssh*, etc.

If you don't have a good grasp of these concepts an excellent place to start would be CompTIA's Network+® program or the ICND-1 portion of Cisco's Cisco Certified Network Associate (CCNA)® program. With a good grasp of the fundamentals you'll be able to secure MikroTik networks.

Using This Book

This book is formatted to highlight important concepts, notes, "quick wins", and common tasks that I've encountered with my own networks and customers. Commands are set apart in a different font so you can easily distinguish what to use at the prompt. This command sets the device hostname:

```
/system identity set name=my-router
```

Longer commands are often split into two parts and may break from one line to the next:

```
/ip firewall filter
add chain=input protocol=tcp dst-port=80 action=accept
    comment="HTTP"
```

Notes call out important knowledge items or answers to frequently asked questions.

> **NOTE**: I am a note, please read me!

Warnings call your attention to commands or common mistakes that could cause loss of services or connectivity. They may also highlight best practices that can protect your networks from security risks or non-compliance with common standards.

> ⚠ **WARNING**: This command will reboot the router!

Making Changes Safely

This book's purpose is to walk you through securing RouterOS devices. To do this we'll be turning off services, configuring the firewall, changing user credentials, and more. Many of these changes can cut you off from a remote device while configuration is in progress. To help prevent you from being cut-off I strongly suggest invoking Safe Mode before making any changes.

Preface

Any changes made in Safe Mode are reverted if your router connection terminates abruptly or if you exit Winbox or console sessions without first leaving Safe Mode. This ensures that any breaking changes made while configuring a device are removed so you can access the device again and troubleshoot. Losing connection while making configuration changes could affect the network's *availability* in a negative way.

> **NOTE**: It's much easier to enter Safe Mode now than it is to lock yourself out of a device and try to find a way back in to undo the latest changes.

Winbox Safe Mode

To enter Safe Mode using Winbox simply click the *Safe Mode* button, as shown in Figure 1. Once clicked the Safe Mode box will turn gray, an indication that you're in Safe Mode as shown in Figure 2.

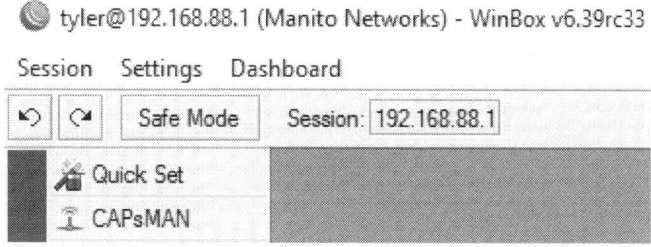

Figure 1: Winbox Safe Mode

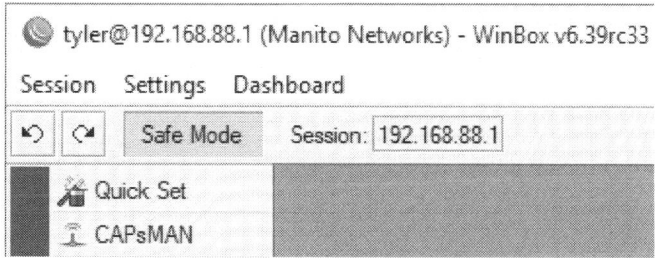

Figure 2: Winbox Safe Mode Engaged

Changes you make on the router will be applied but if you exit Winbox without clicking the Safe Mode box again a warning will pop-up. The dialog that Winbox shows to help you not lose configuration changes is shown in Figure 3 on page xii.

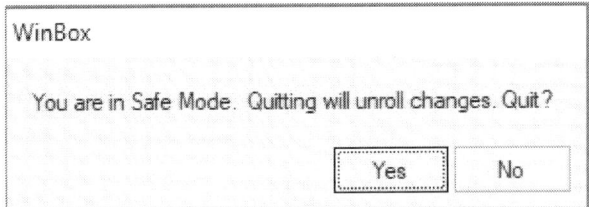

Figure 3: Winbox Quit Warning

To save your changes click the Safe Mode button again to disengage it, and your changes will remain on the device.

Command Line Safe Mode

Safe Mode in the command line environment works almost the same way as in Winbox. To enter Safe Mode at the command line, use the "*Ctrl–X*" keystroke. The prompt will change to indicate you're in Safe Mode as shown in Figure 4.

```
[admin@MikroTik] > [Ctrl-X]
[Safe Mode taken]
[admin@MikroTik] <SAFE>
```

Figure 4: Command Line Safe Mode

To exit Safe Mode and save your changes use the "*Ctrl-X*" keystroke again. To exit the console and abandon your changes use the "*Ctrl-D*" keystroke. Your changes will be abandoned if you are disconnected abruptly as well. Prior to exiting Safe Mode if you want to review pending changes you can use the following command and look for any commands marked with an "*F*" flag:

```
/system history print
```

An example is shown in Figure 5 where the router hostname was changed in Safe Mode, then the recent changes listed.

```
[admin@MikroTik] <SAFE> /system identity set name=router
[admin@router] <SAFE> /system history print
Flags: U - undoable, R - redoable, F - floating-undo
ACTION                         BY        POLICY
F    system identity changed   admin     write
U    package channel changed   admin     write
...
[admin@router] <SAFE> _
```

Figure 5: Safe Mode Undo Changes

The individual change that set the hostname could be rolled back by the "*/undo*" command. Using "*Ctrl-D*" to close the console session will force RouterOS abandon all changes made in Safe Mode as well.

Recommendations

There are a few small recommendations I suggest you follow while securing your MikroTik networks. Some of them are especially important if devices are remote or not easily accessible. Consider the following:

1. Use Safe Mode consistently
2. Test changes on a workbench unit first so you understand the results of each configuration change before applying in production
3. Schedule an outage or maintenance window before reconfiguring production devices
4. Communicate your changes to other network or support staff ahead of time
5. Make small, incremental changes so if something goes wrong it's easy to identify and roll back

None of these recommendations require investment in additional tools or training, and they can save you time and money in the long-run. If your responsibilities include training or mentoring MikroTik professionals these are good habits to help them develop as well.

Chapter 1

Physical Security

Physical security controls are important like firewalls and IPS appliances but they get much less attention in many organizations. Physical destruction or theft can be just as devastating as a hacked device or sabotaged configuration. These individual steps and components secure the physical device before moving on to software and services:

1. List, comment, and disable network ports
2. Enable loop protection
3. Secure the LCD touchscreen
4. Secure the console port
5. Evaluate the security of the physical space

These are the first layers in our defense-in-depth solution for the network.

Securing Router Interfaces

To begin we'll disable any physical network interfaces that aren't in use. This denies an intruder access to the device if they somehow get into the wiring closet or server room. An attacker would have to disconnect a live connection and create the following to plug into the router:

1. A network outage that affects users
2. Conditions that attract the attention of network administrators
3. Interface Up / Down alerts in a centralized network monitoring system (p. 104)

Fortunately, in networks that change very little this task only needs to be done once. If a port needs to be enabled it only takes a moment to execute the single command required.

List Router Interfaces

List all the router's interfaces with the command in Figure 1.1, making note of the names and numbers associated with each interface:

```
[admin@MikroTik] > /interface print
Flags: D - dynamic, X - disabled, R - running, S - slave
 #     NAME             TYPE          ACTUAL-MTU  L2MTU
 0     ether1           ether               1500   1600
 1   S ether2-master    ether               1500   1598
 2   S ether3           ether               1500   1598
 3   S ether4           ether               1500   1598
 4   S ether5           ether               1500   1598
 5  RS wlan1            wlan                1500   1600
 6   R ;;; defconf
bridge                  bridge              1500   1598
[admin@MikroTik] > _
```

Figure 1.1: Listing Interfaces

By default, the interfaces don't have comments to help you distinguish what can be turned off without breaking the network. We'll add interface comments that tell administrators at-a-glance what each interface does. The following commands add comments for *ether1*, *ether2*, *wlan1*, and *bridge* interfaces:

```
/interface ethernet
set ether1 comment=WAN
set ether2 comment="LAN master port"

/interface wireless
set wlan1 comment="Corp wireless"

/interface bridge
set bridge comment="WLAN and LAN bridge"
```

Comments like these will help steer us away from disabling the wrong interfaces in the next section. Once again this is a task that will probably only need to be done a single time. If you have a lot of devices in the field already without interface comments it's easy to update one or two devices a week when you have a moment.

Disable Unused Interfaces

Disable all interfaces that aren't live so they can't be used to access the device. In our case all interfaces except *ether4* and *ether5* are either in use currently or will be. Disable interfaces *ether4* and *ether5* with the following command:

```
/interface set ether4,ether5 disabled=yes
```

Figure 1.2 shows the interfaces with their new comments and *ether4* and *ether5* disabled:

```
[admin@MikroTik] > /interface print
Flags: D - dynamic, X - disabled, R - running, S - slave
 #      NAME           TYPE      ACTUAL-MTU   L2MTU
 0      ;;; WAN
        ether1         ether     1500         1600
 1    S ;;; LAN master port
        ether2-master  ether     1500         1598
 2    S ether3         ether     1500         1598
 3   XS ether4         ether     1500         1598
 4   XS ether5         ether     1500         1598
 5   RS ;;; Corp wireless
        wlan1          wlan      1500         1600
 6    R ;;; WLAN and LAN bridge
        bridge         bridge    1500         1598
[admin@MikroTik] > _
```

Figure 1.2: Disabled Interfaces

The status of *ether4* and *ether5* are shown with an "X" indicating they can't be used to connect to the device and its networks. The following command would disable any interface not currently running. While it can be useful to do this programmatically be careful to verify it's typed correctly:

```
/interface ethernet set [find where !running] disabled=yes
```

> **NOTE:** The ! symbol used above means "*NOT*". This */interface ethernet* command will not disable wireless or other virtual interfaces.

Both methods of disabling interfaces ensure that even if an attacker gets physical access to your device they won't be able to get in via those ports. To get local access to the network an attacker would have to first remove a live connection and hopefully trigger an alerting system.

Loop Protection

Disabling unused ports can protect the *confidentiality* of the network but it does little to ensure its *availability*. A network loop on user-facing ports could cause a loss of services when a loop is created with switches or hubs. The Loop Protect feature monitors interfaces for excessive broadcast traffic and shuts them down if a loop is suspected. Since *ether2* and *ether3* are user-facing ports the feature gets enabled on them with the following commands:

```
/interface ethernet
set ether2 loop-protect=on
set ether3 loop-protect=on
```

Interfaces will be disabled by default for five minutes when a loop is suspected. While this would cut off the hosts connected to that interface it also isolates the broadcast storm. Hopefully users aren't plugging hubs or switches into the network but just in case it's good to use this feature.

LCD Touchscreen

Some RouterBoards like the RB2011, RB3011, CRS, and CCR models feature an LCD screen. This screen can be used to monitor a device locally, configure interfaces, and modify other limited settings. If an attacker has local access to a device and the LCD screen hasn't been secured this could create several security issues.

LCD Touchscreen PIN

The default PIN code to access the system and make changes via the LCD is "*1234*". This information about the default PIN is freely-available on the internet and "*1234*" is easily guessable. If you want to keep the device accessible via the LCD screen set a non-default PIN. Avoid the following number combinations when choosing a PIN:

- Birth dates or years
- The location's street number[1]
- Number sequences (1234, 9876, 2468, etc.)
- Number pad patterns (four corners, etc.)

The following command sets the PIN to "*1642*":

```
/lcd pin set pin-number=1642
```

---

[1] I have had some success with cipher locks and PIN pads during on-site audits using street, building, and room numbers. Don't use these numbers!

> ⚠ **WARNING**: If an attacker can log into a RouterOS device the PIN will be visible via the *"/lcd pin print"* command.

PIN Hide

If you're using a PIN to access the LCD screen it's possible to hide the PIN as it's being entered. This behavior is like how an ATM hides your bank card PIN on the screen as it's entered. Hiding the PIN can prevent an attacker from "shoulder surfing" and learning the PIN. Use the following command to hide the PIN numbers as they are being entered on the screen:

```
/lcd pin set hide-pin-number=yes
```

Read-Only

Setting the LCD screen to read-only allows you to monitor the device via the LCD but not make changes. If you aren't concerned about someone seeing interface performance or IP addresses via the LCD this is a good mode to be in.

```
/lcd set read-only-mode=yes
```

> **NOTE**: The PIN does not apply when the LCD is in read-only mode.

LCD Disable

It's possible to disable the LCD screen entirely. Even if another PIN hasn't been set if the screen is disabled the device can't be accessed. Even if you decide to disable LCD screens entirely you should first set a PIN. This ensures that if someone months or years later decides to re-enable the screens they won't be vulnerable to the default PIN. Disable the LCD screen using the following command:

```
/lcd screen set disabled-yes
```

Console Port

An attacker with physical access to the router could leverage the console port if your device model (e.g. CCR, CRS, etc.) has one. To check if your router has a hardware console port use the following command:

```
/system console print
```

Serial console ports will be labeled as *serialN* where *N* is the port number. An example in Winbox is shown in Figure 1.3.

```
[admin@MikroTik] > /system console print
Flags: X - disabled, W - wedged, U - used, F - free
 #    PORT           VCNO        TERM
 0 F  serial0                    vt102
 1 U                 1           linux
 2 F                 2           linux
 3 F                 3           linux
 4 F                 4           linux
 5 F                 5           linux
 6 F                 6           linux
 7 F                 7           linux
 8 F                 8           linux
[admin@MikroTik] > _
```

Figure 1.3: Console Ports

If you're not using the console port it may be best to disable it. Use the following command to disable the *serial0* port (port number 0):

```
/system console set 0 disabled=yes
```

If you want to limit the amount of simultaneous virtual console connections into the device you can also disable the higher-numbered *linux*-type items. There are eight available virtual console connections and the first is marked as in-use with a "*U*". This connection is me logged in via SSH to run the "*/system console print*" command so you see the results in Figure 1.3.

Physical Device Security

During some audits I've performed it was not surprising to find devices out in the open and accessible. If they were in a wiring closet or mechanical space they often weren't behind a locked door. Many commercial and organizational spaces aren't built-out with the physical security of IT equipment in mind. This is made more difficult in buildings with shared wiring closets or mechanical rooms where multiple tenants have equipment located with hand-offs from service providers. These spaces may be locked but it's often difficult to know everyone who has a key. I recommend the following controls be put in place if possible to secure your physical devices:

- Secure devices in a locking rack, either wall-mounted or floor-mounted.
- In lieu of a locking rack, secure devices to a wooden backboard with the included hardware.
- Disable physical interfaces not in use (p. 3).
- Locate equipment in spaces protected by a keyed door or cipher-lock.
- Monitor space access with security cameras or on-site security personnel.
- Periodically audit who has access to the spaces your devices occupy.
- Check to verify that no documentation or notes have been left around or attached to a device.

If robust physical controls can't be put in place then logical controls like robust passwords, device monitoring, port disabling, and others become even more important.

Chapter 2

Software & Services

With the physical device and ports secured we'll turn to securing the software on the device. Assuming there isn't an insider threat with physical access to the device most attacks will occur remotely via the ports and protocols running by default. The following steps will secure software on the device:

1. List and disable software packages
2. Scan the device and identify open ports
3. Disable unsecure and unencrypted services
4. Secure access to DNS
5. Turn off or restrict MAC services
6. Disable services that aren't used day-to-day
7. Enable robust SSH encryption
8. Regenerate new SSH keys
9. Remove the default public SNMP access
10. Secure the SMB service
11. Disable the SOCKS proxy

Each part of this list contributes to our overall defense-in-depth approach. On top of these changes, guidance on page 97 ensures that the latest stable release of RouterOS is running as well.

Securing Software

Directions for running the latest stable version of RouterOS are covered on page 97, but before that it's a good idea to disable unused packages. If a vulnerability is discovered in the latest version of RouterOS affecting a package that isn't running your device remains secure. However, if all default packages are running there's a chance your router could be compromised via a package you're not actively using like Hotspot, Multiprotocol Label Switching (MPLS), Internet Protocol v6 (IPv6), etc.

List Installed Packages

List the RouterOS packages currently installed with the "*/system package print*" command as shown in Figure 2.1.

```
[admin@MikroTik] > /system package print
Flags: X - disabled
 #   NAME                VERSION      SCHEDULED
 0   routeros-mipsbe     6.41rc26
 1   system              6.41rc26
 2   ipv6                6.41rc26
 3   wireless            6.41rc26
 4 X hotspot             6.41rc26
 5   dhcp                6.41rc26
 6   mpls                6.41rc26
 7   routing             6.41rc26
 8   ppp                 6.41rc26
 9   security            6.41rc26
10   advanced-tools      6.41rc26
11   multicast           6.41rc26
[admin@MikroTik] > _
```

Figure 2.1: List Packages

In the example above the *Hotspot* package is already disabled. Identify and make a list of the packages you aren't currently using. For a description of what each package does check out the Package documentation in the MikroTik Wiki[1].

---

[1] https://wiki.mikrotik.com/wiki/Manual:System/Packages

Disable Packages

Once you have confirmed you aren't using the functionality of a package, e.g. PPP, go ahead and disable it. The following command disables the *PPP* package:

```
[admin@MikroTik] > /system package disable ppp
[admin@MikroTik] > /system package print
Flags: X - disabled
 #     NAME              VERSION      SCHEDULED
 0     routeros-mipsbe   6.41rc26
 1     system            6.41rc26
 2     ipv6              6.41rc26
 3     wireless          6.41rc26
 4  X  hotspot           6.41rc26
 5     dhcp              6.41rc26
 6     mpls              6.41rc26
 7     routing           6.41rc26
 8     ppp               6.41rc26     scheduled for disable
 9     security          6.41rc26
10     advanced-tools    6.41rc26
11     multicast         6.41rc26
[admin@MikroTik] > _
```

Figure 2.2: Disabling RouterOS Package

A reboot is required to complete the process started by the commands above. Since a reboot is required to disable packages it's important to accomplish this step during router provisioning. Disabling packages while the device is on the workbench and not moving production traffic is the best way to do it.

Securing Services

Services running on the router create much of the device's attack surface. Several services like File Transfer Protocol (FTP) are not secure, and many services are running out of-the-box even though you won't use them much of the time or at all. Port scanners and attackers performing reconnaissance on your networks will use those services to fingerprint your devices and identify "soft targets" to attempt access. Any weak or default passwords you might have in place can be leveraged over those protocols and services to exploit your networks. Table 2.1 on the next page shows the typical IP services that can run on the router and which are enabled by default.

Service	Protocol	Port	Default Enabled	Page
API	TCP	8728	X	32
API-SSL	TCP	8729	X	32
Bandwidth Test	TCP	2000	X	26
DNS	TCP, UDP	53	–	21
FTP	TCP	20, 21	X	32
NTP	UDP	123	–	100
SMB	TCP	445	–	106
SNMP	UDP	161	–	33
SSH	TCP	22	X	28
Telnet	TCP	23	X	–
UPnP	TCP	2828	–	36
Winbox	TCP	8291	X	33
WWW	TCP	80	X	–
WWW-SSL	TCP	443	X	–
SOCKS	TCP	1080	–	37
DHCP	UDP	67	X	–

Table 2.1: Router Services

Network Scan with Nmap

In this book we use the Nmap network scanner[2] to probe our router and discover running services on open ports. Nmap is a mainstay of the network security community and learning Nmap is a worthwhile endeavor. If you don't already have Nmap installed use the following sections to get started.

> ⚠ **WARNING**: Due to its popularity with hackers, auditors, and network professionals alike there have been attempts to distribute malware[a] in fake Nmap downloads. **Only download Nmap from the official `Nmap.org` website, or install from official Linux package repositories.**
>
> [a] http://insecure.org/news/download-com-fiasco.html

Microsoft Windows

Download Nmap from the official Nmap.org download page for Microsoft Windows at the following URL:

https://nmap.org/download.html#windows

---
[2] https://nmap.org/

Run the installer to install Nmap and the graphical front-end Zenmap. The same Linux *nmap* command options used on page 13 are used in Zenmap.

Linux

The Nmap scanner is available on all major Linux platforms. Use APT or YUM package managers depending on your distribution to install Nmap:

```
sudo apt-get install zenmap        # Ubuntu / Debian
yum install nmap nmap-frontend     # CentOS, RHEL, SUSE, etc.
```

The *Zenmap* package provides a graphical front-end for the Nmap scanner on Linux as well. On Microsoft Windows installations it's automatically included as part of the binary installer package.

Network Discovery Scan

With Nmap installed we can do a scan to determine what services are running on the router. This will be our starting point for securing the router and limiting the attack surface. Open the Zenmap GUI as shown in Figure 2.3.

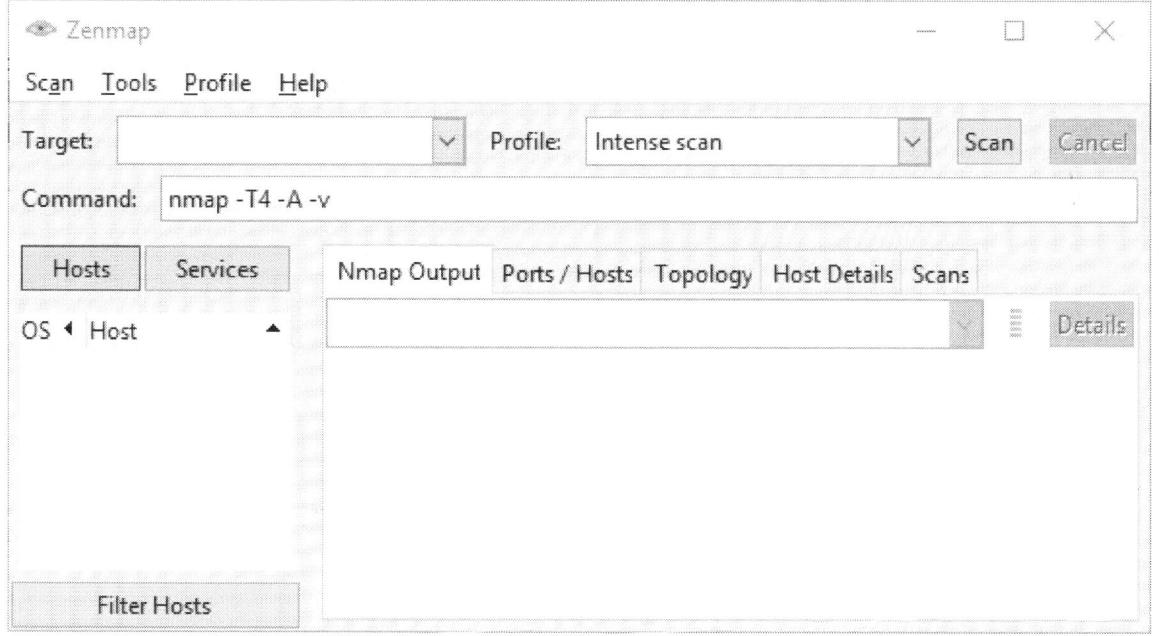

Figure 2.3: Zenmap Open

Copy the following command and paste it into the *Command* field:

```
nmap -sT -sU -p 1-65535 -T4 -A -v --open 192.168.88.1
```

The following options are used in the scan command:

- *–sT*: Perform a TCP Connect scan
- *–sU*: Perform a UDP scan
- *–p 1–65535*: Scan ports one through 65535 since RouterOS uses some less-common ports in the upper range
- *–T4*: The speed of the scan (T1 is slowest, T5 is extremely fast)
- *–A*: Enable OS and service detection
- *–v*: Increase verbosity so you can watch the scan run
- *--open*: Only show open or possibly open ports to keep the output from becoming cluttered
- *192.168.88.1*: The default MikroTik IP address, adjust as necessary for your environment.

On Linux open a Terminal and copy-paste the same command shown above. Nmap with the Zenmap front-end ready to run the scan is shown in Figure 2.4.

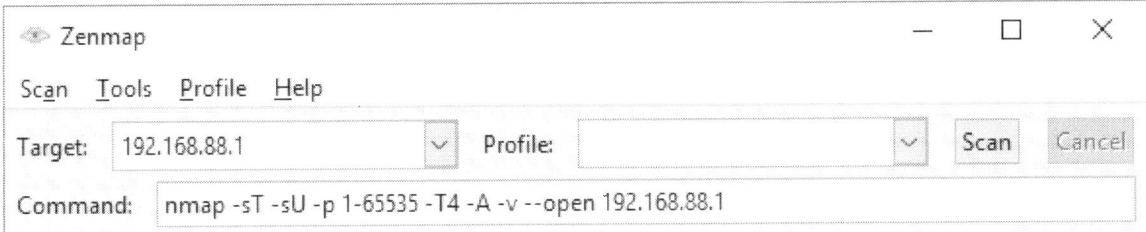

Figure 2.4: Microsoft Windows Nmap Scan

Click *Scan* to begin the port scanning process. This will take some time to complete and the verbose option will show regular estimates of the remaining time. Scanning UDP ports takes a particularly long time because of the nature of the protocol. Figure 2.5 on the following page shows some of the long scan output once it's finished:

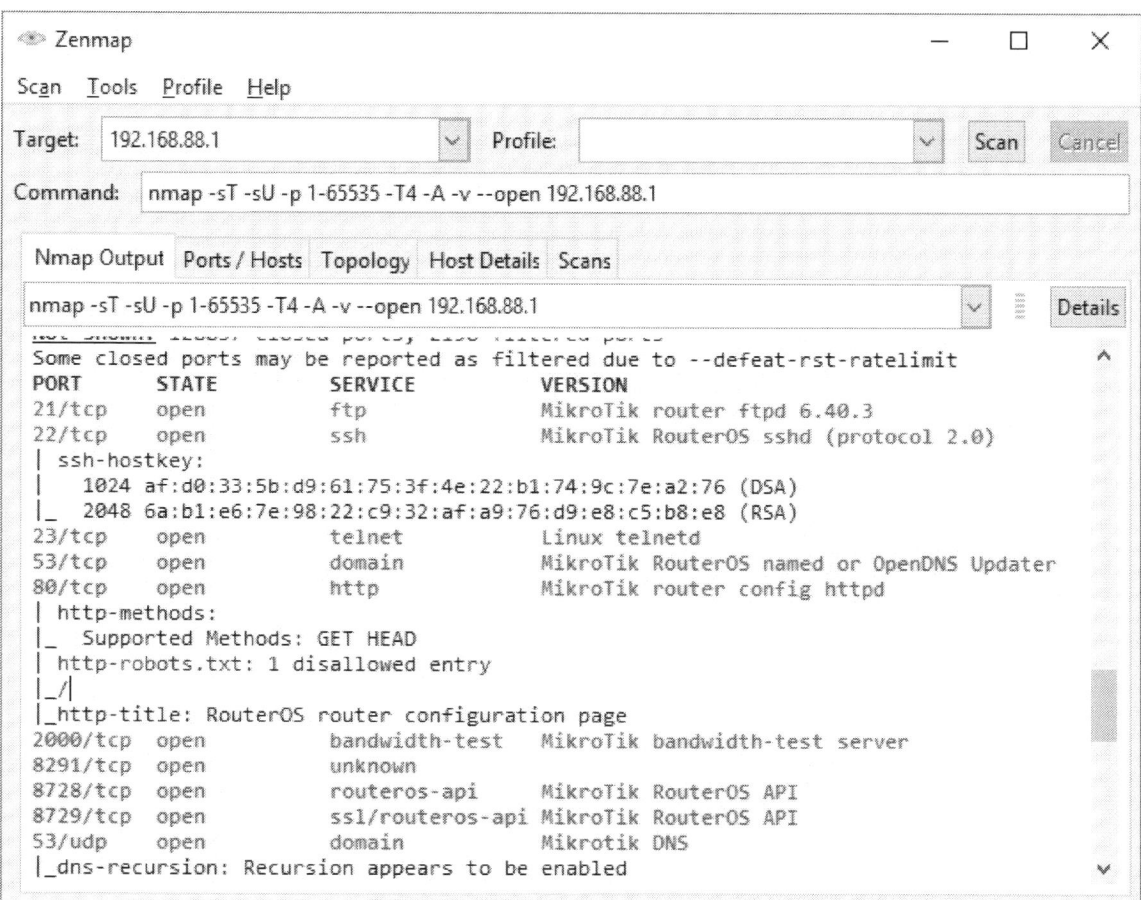

Figure 2.5: Completed Nmap Scan

Discovered Ports

Expanding the *Services* tab on the left side of the Zenmap window allows you to easily scroll through the discovered ports discussed in the next section. Figure 2.6 shows a consolidated list of the open ports that were discovered open during the Nmap scan:

```
Discovered open port 53/udp on 192.168.88.1
Discovered open port 80/tcp on 192.168.88.1
Discovered open port 23/tcp on 192.168.88.1
Discovered open port 53/tcp on 192.168.88.1
Discovered open port 21/tcp on 192.168.88.1
Discovered open port 22/tcp on 192.168.88.1
Discovered open port 2000/tcp on 192.168.88.1
Discovered open port 8729/tcp on 192.168.88.1
Discovered open port 8291/tcp on 192.168.88.1
Discovered open port 8728/tcp on 192.168.88.1
```

Figure 2.6: Discovered Open Ports

While it's great for initial setup that the router is very accessible out-of-the-box it isn't an appropriate long-term security posture. By turning off services that aren't in use or are unsecure we can reduce the overall attack surface.

Discovered Services

Figure 2.7 shows the ports and services discovered during the scan. Your results may differ slightly depending the software version and any changes made from the factory default. MikroTik does make changes to the default configuration periodically as well which may affect your baseline scan.

```
PORT         STATE       SERVICE           VERSION
21/tcp       open        ftp               MikroTik router ftpd
   6.40.3
22/tcp       open        ssh               MikroTik RouterOS sshd
   ...
23/tcp       open        telnet            Linux telnetd
53/tcp       open        domain            MikroTik RouterOS named
   ...
80/tcp       open        http              MikroTik router config
   httpd
8291/tcp     open        unknown
8728/tcp     open        routeros-api      MikroTik RouterOS API
8729/tcp     open        ssl/routeros-api  MikroTik RouterOS API
53/udp       open        domain            Mikrotik DNS
```

Figure 2.7: Service Scan Results

The *Services* tab in Zenmap gives more in-depth details about each service if available as shown in Figure 2.8 on the following page:

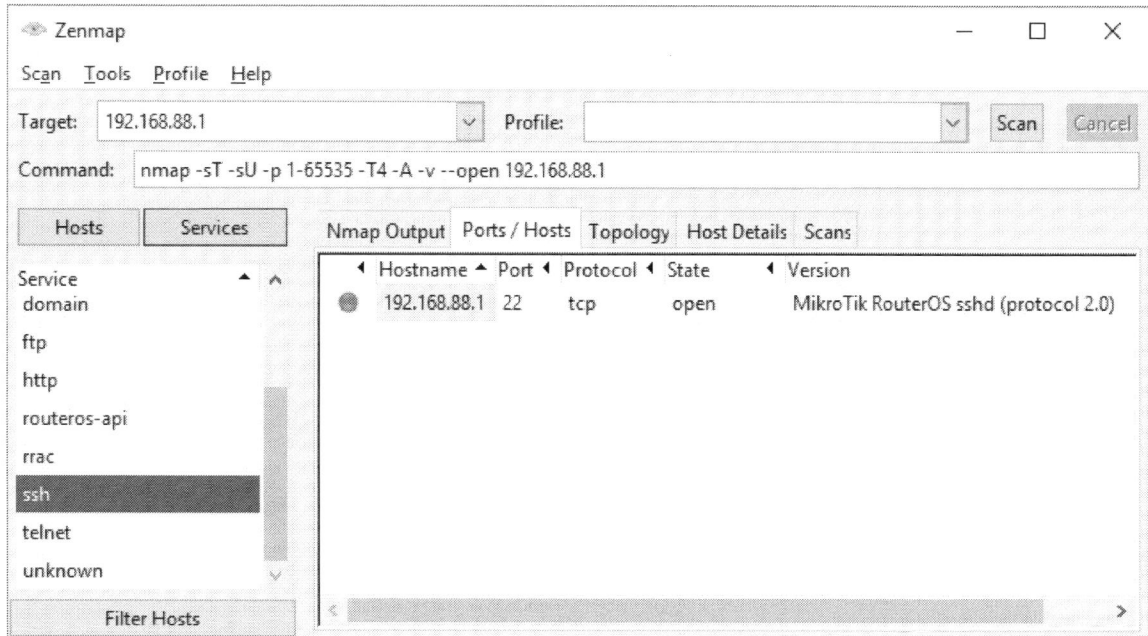

Figure 2.8: Zenmap Services View

Scan Summary

Based on the results of the scan there are multiple issues that need to be remediated:

1. Unencrypted protocols are running

2. Services that can impact network performance like Bandwidth Test are running

3. Remote configuration services are running and reachable from the port scan device

These issues need to be fixed before going any further due to their severity. Given that we're running factory default credentials there is a good chance this router could be compromised soon after being brought online via any number of these services.

Securing IP Services

For the purposes of this guide the router will only be administered through SSH and Secure-mode Winbox. Both SSH and Winbox sessions are encrypted so we don't have to worry about plaintext information leaking, and this is in-line with current best practices. SSH can also be used in place of FTP for transferring files to and from the router, so there isn't much reason to leave FTP running. To begin we'll view running services on the router then shut off all services except SSH and Winbox. At the end we'll scan the router again and verify the results of our configuration changes.

View IP Services

List services running on the router as shown in Figure 2.9.

```
[admin@MikroTik] > /ip service print
Flags: X - disabled, I - invalid
 #    NAME            PORT    ADDRESS         CERTIFICATE
 0    telnet          23
 1    ftp             21
 2    www             80
 3    ssh             22
 4 XI www-ssl         443                     none
 5    api             8728
 6    winbox          8291
 7    api-ssl         8729                    none
[admin@MikroTik] >
```

Figure 2.9: IP Services

The *HTTPS* service has been disabled by default in recent releases of RouterOS. If your organization has its own HTTPS certificates they can be imported and used on RouterOS devices.

Disable IP Services

We'll turn off most of the IP services that RouterOS can run to reduce the device's attack surface. Some network administrators attempt to secure services by changing the default port numbers, implementing "security by obscurity". While this might delay an attacker for a short while it is **not an effective defense** as the port scan will show. Nmap and other tools will quickly identify running services even if the ports are changed. Service should be disabled if they meet these criteria:

1. The service is unsecure and a secure alternative is available

2. The service isn't used in day-to-day system administration

3. No bona fide reason exists for keeping the service enabled

The following commands turn off unsecure services to reduce attack surface:

```
/ip service
disable telnet
disable ftp
disable www
disable api
```

The following commands turn off services that, while encrypted, may not be used for day-to-day administration in most networks:

```
/ip service
disable www-ssl
disable api-ssl
```

These services in both sets of commands could be disabled in one comma-separated line but I've split them out so they can be checked off one-by-one. Disabling HTTP specifically satisfies Infrastructure Router STIG Finding V-3085:

> "Network devices must have HTTP service for administrative access disabled."

Using HTTPS instead of HTTP is acceptable but the HTTPS portal should only be available from trusted subnets or management hosts. FTP must be disabled per Infrastructure Router STIG Finding V-14668:

> "FTP servers on the device must be disabled."

Verify that the basic services have been disabled and display with an "X" by the service name. Use the command shown in Figure 2.10 to verify the unused or unsecure services are disabled:

```
[admin@MikroTik] > /ip service print
Flags: X - disabled, I - invalid
 #   NAME         PORT  ADDRESS      CERTIFICATE
 0 XI telnet      23
 1 XI ftp         21
 2 XI www         80
 3    ssh         22
 4 XI www-ssl     443                none
 5 XI api         8728
 6    winbox      8291
 7 XI api-ssl     8729               none
[admin@MikroTik] > _
```

Figure 2.10: Disabled IP Services

Access to the remaining secure protocols can also be restricted to a subnet or specific management host. If an organization has IT staff in their own management VLAN this can provide another layer in the defense-in-depth strategy. Limit access to Winbox and SSH on the router to the *192.168.90.0/24* management network with the following commands:

```
/ip service
set ssh address=192.168.90.0/24
set winbox address=192.168.90.0/24
```

Figure 2.11 shows the result of the additional settings:

```
[admin@MikroTik] > /ip service print
Flags: X - disabled, I - invalid
 #   NAME         PORT    ADDRESS
 0 XI telnet      23
 1 XI ftp         21
 2 XI www         80
 3    ssh         22      192.168.90.0/24
 4 XI www-ssl     443
 5 XI api         8728
 6    winbox      8291    192.168.90.0/24
 7 XI api-ssl    8729
[admin@MikroTik] > _
```

Figure 2.11: Management Subnet for Services

DNS

The default configuration for RouterOS allows for remote DNS queries to the router. The default configuration is shown in Figure 2.12:

```
[admin@MikroTik] > /ip dns print
                 servers:
         dynamic-servers:
    allow-remote-requests: yes
       max-udp-packet-size: 4096
      query-server-timeout: 2s
       query-total-timeout: 10s
    max-concurrent-queries: 100
max-concurrent-tcp-sessions: 20
                cache-size: 2048KiB
             cache-max-ttl: 1w
                cache-used: 14KiB
[admin@MikroTik] > _
```

Figure 2.12: Default DNS Configuration

Recursion is also enabled by default when the Domain Name Service (DNS) service is running. This is shown in an Nmap port scan result snippet in Figure 2.13:

```
53/udp    open   domain?
|_dns-recursion: Recursion appears to be enabled
```

Figure 2.13: DNS Recursion Enabled

As of this writing there is no way to disable recursive lookups via the router. The router also comes pre-configured with a static name record for "*router.lan*" that resolves to *192.168.88.1* as shown in Figure 2.14:

```
[admin@MikroTik] > /ip dns static print
Flags: D - dynamic, X - disabled
 #    NAME         REGEXP        ADDRESS         TTL
 0    router.lan                 192.168.88.1    1d
[admin@MikroTik] > _
```

Figure 2.14: Default Static DNS Entry

If the router isn't your DNS server then we shouldn't be allowing DNS requests. Chances are in enterprise environments there are ISC BIND or Microsoft Windows Active Directory servers running the DNS role. If that's the case then disable DNS lookups via the router using the following command:

```
/ip dns set allow-remote-requests=no
```

Routers that respond to DNS queries from all sources (known as open resolvers) can be co-opted into DNS Amplification DDoS attacks[3]. This allows attacks to be perpetrated using your own devices and hampers the *availability* of your networks. Not running an open resolver is part of being a good neighbor on the internet.

If you're using the router as a DNS server then firewall rules should be put in place to prevent abuse of the service. The chapter on firewalls (p. 45) will guide you through building firewall rules. Use an *input* chain rule (p. 47) to allow DNS queries from trusted subnets and block all others.

Neighbor Discovery

While neighbor discovery is a very useful tool for administrators it's also a huge source of information for attackers. Figure 2.15 shows the device details available via neighbor discovery on a factory-default router without being logged in:

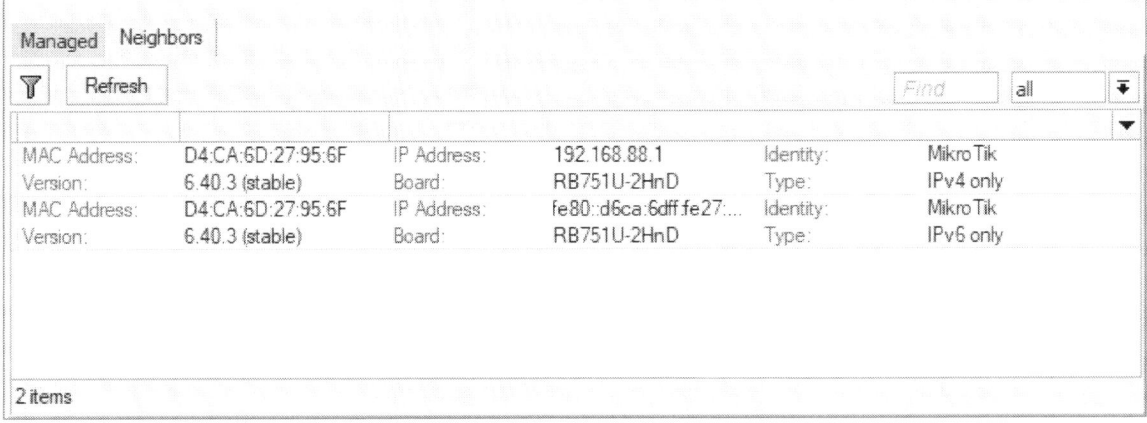

Figure 2.15: Neighbor Discovery Information

The Board (model) and MAC address information shown in Winbox match a sticker on the bottom or back of most RouterBOARD units. This information could be leveraged by an attacker using social engineering because these details would only be known by a trusted insider with access to the device. Little do the victims know that it's trivial to get this information from a MikroTik-based guest wireless network available from the parking lot or lobby area. Figure 2.16 on the following page shows the default ND configuration:

---

[3] https://www.us-cert.gov/ncas/alerts/TA13-088A

```
[admin@MikroTik] > /ip neighbor discovery settings print
default: yes
default-for-dynamic: no
[admin@MikroTik] > _
```

Figure 2.16: Default Neighbor Discovery Configuration

The default RouterOS configuration was updated recently to disable ND on the *ether1* WAN port. However, it's still running on all other interfaces as shown in Figure 2.17:

```
[admin@MikroTik] > /ip neighbor discovery print
Flags: X - disabled
 #    NAME
 0 X  ether1
 1    ether2-master
 2    ether3
 3    ether4
 4    ether5
 5    wlan1
 6    ;;; defconf
bridge
[admin@MikroTik] > _
```

Figure 2.17: Interfaces Running Neighbor Discovery

An all-around best practice is to disable MikroTik Neighbor Discovery Protocol (NDP) on non–management interfaces. This will stop the router from being discovered by other devices running MikroTik NDP or Cisco Discovery Protocol (CDP).

IPv4-ND

First, we'll turn ND off by default for IPv4 so when new interfaces come online they won't participate:

```
/ip neighbor discovery settings
set default=no default-for-dynamic=no
```

Then we'll shut IPv4 ND off on each individual interface that's already running. This is especially important for WISP organizations who are using MikroTik devices as CPEs. Depending on a WISP's architecture (bridged vs. routed, client isolation configuration, etc.) having ND running on customer-premise equipment could disclose information about one customer to another. Disable IPv4 ND on all interfaces with the following command:

```
/ip neighbor discovery set [find] discover=no
```

Use the same command in Figure 2.17 on the previous page to list ND interfaces:

```
[admin@MikroTik] > /ip neighbor discovery print
Flags: X - disabled
 #   NAME
 0 X ether1
 1 X ether2-master
 2 X ether3
 3 X ether4
 4 X ether5
 5 X wlan1
 6 X ;;; defconf
bridge
[admin@MikroTik] > _
```

Figure 2.18: Disabled Neighbor Discovery Interfaces

If you have a management network it wouldn't hurt to allow discovery protocols to run just on that network's interface. The following command enables neighbor discovery on management interface *vlan100*:

```
/ip neighbor discovery set vlan100 discover=yes
```

IPv6 Neighbor Discovery

Unlike in IPv4-only networks ND plays important roles in provisioning IPv6 addresses within your dual-stack environments. From MikroTik's IPv6 ND documentation[4]:

> "Neighbor Discovery (ND) is a set of messages and processes that determine relationships between neighboring nodes. ND, compared to IPv4, replaces Address Resolution Protocol (ARP), Internet Control Message Protocol (ICMP) Router Discovery, and ICMP Redirect and provides additional functionality."

We can't disable IPv6 ND wholesale for these reasons without breaking your dual-stack networks. I also hesitate to recommend selectively disabling it on interfaces without bench-testing the effects on your IPv6 hosts because there are multiple ways of provisioning IPv6 addresses (prefix delegation and DHCPv6). With this new reliance on ND for IPv6 it will be important to rely on other controls like firewalls to limit attacker's reconnaissance attempts.

---

[4]https://wiki.mikrotik.com/wiki/Manual:IPv6/ND#Neighbor_discovery

MAC Services

MAC services allow you to make connections to RouterOS devices without an assigned IP address. Unfortunately, these services are turned on by default and running on almost all interfaces. Figure 2.19 shows MAC-Server running on the local *bridge* interface that's connected to all wireless and wired ports except for the WAN:

```
[admin@MikroTik] > /tool mac-server print
Flags: X - disabled, * - default
#     INTERFACE
0 X*  all
1     bridge
[admin@MikroTik] > _
```

Figure 2.19: MAC-Server Defaults

In RouterOS it's not possible to remove the default entry for *all* so we'll leave it disabled. Use the following commands to disable all instances of the various MAC services:

```
/tool mac-server
set [find] disabled=yes
mac-winbox set [find] disabled=yes
ping set enabled=no
```

Verify that the other services have been disabled (shown with an "X" by the service name) by running the following:

```
/tool mac-server
print
mac-winbox print
ping print
```

Re-enable MAC services on the dedicated management interface *vlan100* with the following commands:

```
/tool mac-server
add interface=vlan100 disabled=no
mac-winbox add interface=vlan100 disabled=no
```

Bandwidth Test Server

The Bandwidth Test functionality is very handy when testing network throughput and reliability. However, this feature will saturate a network link in the process of testing which can take down a production network. If an attacker is familiar with MikroTik they will know about this built-in tool and leverage it to compromise your *availability*.

> **NOTE**: I recommend only using this tool to test network segments in a lab or after verifying the network can tolerate some amount of outage. This tool will saturate a network link and can cause your router's CPU to hit 100% during testing like in Figure 2.20.

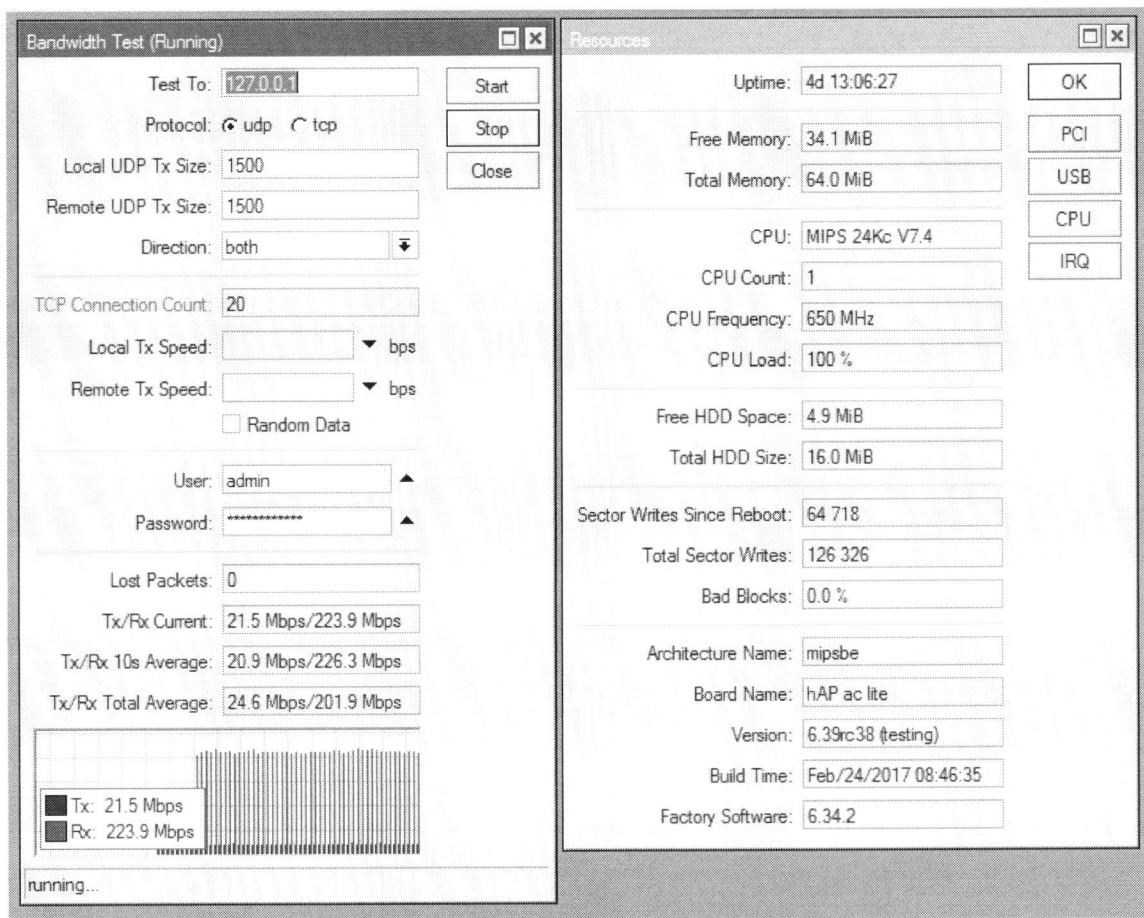

Figure 2.20: Bandwidth Test 100% CPU

Disable the Bandwidth Test Server when not in use with the following command:

```
/tool bandwidth-server
set enabled=no authenticate=yes
```

If you're using the Bandwidth Test functionality be sure to verify that authentication is enabled when the feature is turned on. The Winbox dialog in Figure 2.21 shows the *Authenticate* box checked. This option should always be checked even when the feature is disabled, so if in the future you re-enable it there will still be protections in place.

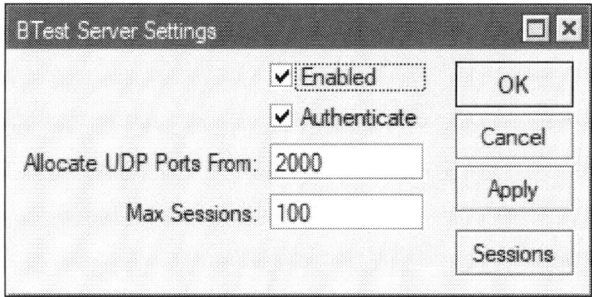

Figure 2.21: Bandwidth Test Server Authentication

⚠**WARNING**: You must update the default *admin* credential along with making these changes. Otherwise even with the *Authenticate* box checked an attacker can leverage the factory-default credentials. See page 65 for steps to complete this task.

RoMON

We'll also disable the RoMON feature if you aren't using it to further reduce the attack surface. Use the following command to disable the service:

```
/tool romon set enabled=no
```

For those using RoMON it should be secured first with *secrets* using the following command:

```
/tool romon set secrets=abc123! enabled=yes
```

Figure 2.22 on the next page shows the (abbreviated) results when we enable the service, set a secret, then run discovery with another RoMON router on the network:

```
[admin@MikroTik] > /tool romon print
enabled: yes
id: 00:00:00:00:00:00
secrets: abc123!
current-id: D4:CA:6D:27:95:6E

[admin@MikroTik] > /tool romon discover
Flags: A - active
    ADDRESS            COST    HOPS    VERSION   BOARD
A   6C:3B:6B:05:CB:BE  200     1       6.41rc34  RB952Ui-5
    ac2nD

[admin@MikroTik] > _
```

Figure 2.22: RoMON Service Running

We're still able to take advantage of the overlay network but in a secure manner that doesn't create additional risk.

Remediation Scan

Until we scan the router again there isn't definitive proof that the security issues identified on page 17 have been fixed. A remediation scan run after configuration changes have been made will confirm that the security posture of the router is where we'd like it to be. Run the same scan outlined on page 13 and compare the results. After running the steps in the previous sections these are the new scan results:

```
Scanning router.manitonetworks.com (192.168.88.1) [65535
    ports]
Discovered open port 22/tcp on 192.168.88.1
Discovered open port 8291/tcp on 192.168.88.1
```

Securing SSH

While SSH is a secure protocol with robust encryption it does require some extra configuration. These changes bring networks in-line with recent developments in best practices and industry compliance standards. Many RouterOS administrators aren't aware these configuration options exist because they don't show up in Winbox or Webfig menus. As of this writing all changes made in the next two subsections must be done from the CLI.

Enable Strong Crypto

Stronger crypto for SSH is available as of RouterOS 6.30 so we'll enable that. SSH clients like PuTTY[5] that can utilize the stronger ciphers will default to those and leave the weaker ciphers unused. Routers should only be administered via secure protocols, and those protocols should use robust ciphers per Infrastructure Router STIG Finding V-3069:

> "Management connections to a network device must be established using secure protocols with FIPS 140-2 validated cryptographic modules."

As of this writing there is no way to explicitly disable the weaker ciphers in RouterOS for purposes of SSH Turn on the SSH strong crypto with the following command:

```
/ip ssh set strong-crypto=yes
```

Figure 2.23 shows the strong crypto enabled with the key size of 2048:

```
[admin@MikroTik] > /ip ssh print
forwarding-enabled: no
always-allow-password-login: no
strong-crypto: yes
host-key-size: 2048
[admin@MikroTik] > _
```

Figure 2.23: List SSH Settings

Running the slow, comprehensive port scan shows the full results of the *strong-crypto* option. Figure 2.24 shows the list of available SSH encryption algorithms before the configuration change:

```
|   encryption_algorithms: (9)
|        aes128-ctr
|        aes192-ctr
|        aes256-ctr
|        aes128-cbc
|        aes192-cbc
|        aes256-cbc
|        blowfish-cbc
|        3des-cbc
|        none
```

Figure 2.24: Weak SSH Crypto

---

[5] http://www.chiark.greenend.org.uk/~sgtatham/putty/latest.html

The *none* and *3des* (or Triple-DES as it's known) options shouldn't ever be used in production networks. Figure 2.25 shows the available encryption algorithms after *strong-crypto* is enabled:

```
|    encryption_algorithms: (2)
|        aes256-ctr
|        aes192-ctr
```

Figure 2.25: Strong SSH Crypto

The options for weak or no encryption aren't available, and the lowest possible Advanced Encryption Standard (AES) level is 192-bit. Hashing algorithms get the same treatment as well, with MD5 hashing removed and replaced by SHA2-256.

Regenerate Encryption Keys

When a router is first turned on it generates encryption keys for the host's use. Updated compliance standards require that encryption keys be regenerated before devices go into production. This ensures that if someone got hold of the keys during a vendor's process or in transit they can't be used for Man-in-the-Middle attacks. Use the command shown in Figure 2.26 to create new keys:

```
[admin@MikroTik] > /ip ssh regenerate-host-key
This will regenerate current SSH host keys (changes will take
    affect only after service restart or reboot), yes? [y/N]:
y
12:37:35 echo: ssh,critical SSH host key regenerated, reboot
    or service restart required!
[admin@MikroTik] > /system reboot
```

Figure 2.26: Regenerating SSH Keys

Reboot the device to put the new keys to work securing connections. The next time you connect to the device using PuTTY or another client you should see the dialog box asking you to accept another certificate as shown in Figure 2.27 on the following page:

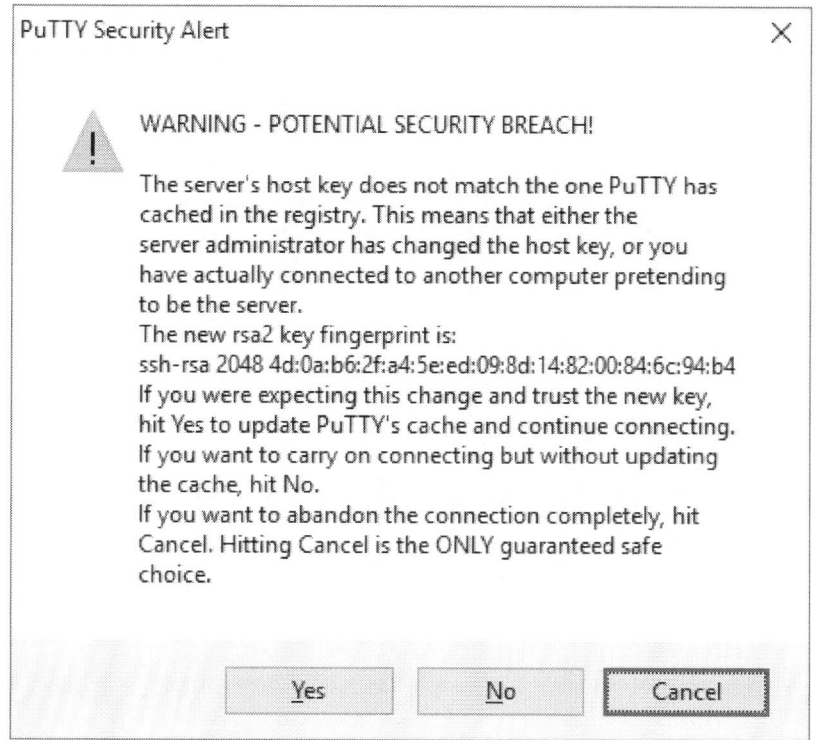

Figure 2.27: PuTTY Security Alert

Port scans before and after the host key regeneration show that the command worked. The following host keys were in-place prior to the command:

```
22/tcp   open  ssh  MikroTik RouterOS sshd (protocol 2.0)
|_banner: SSH-2.0-ROSSSH
| ssh-hostkey:
|   1024 c2:9b:55:c9:57:a3:53:f4:1e:45:1c:83:89:c4:1f:26 (DSA)
|_  2048 62:d0:ad:e6:d7:c0:e0:8d:36:26:93:bc:ad:4c:7a:31 (RSA)
```

Now these keys are being used after the router rebooted:

```
22/tcp   open  ssh  MikroTik RouterOS sshd (protocol 2.0)
|_banner: SSH-2.0-ROSSSH
| ssh-hostkey:
|   1024 af:d0:33:5b:d9:61:75:3f:4e:22:b1:74:9c:7e:a2:76 (DSA)
|_  2048 6a:b1:e6:7e:98:22:c9:32:af:a9:76:d9:e8:c5:b8:e8 (RSA)
```

API Controls

The RouterOS API allows you to do almost everything that an SSH or Winbox connection would allow for in a centralized, programmatic fashion. The API makes configuration functions available to Python, PHP, Go, and other languages. If an organization is using the API services to centralize control and monitoring there's no problem with leaving them enabled. Access should be restricted, however, to the centralized resources that are using API access. The following commands enable the API services and restrict their access to the dedicated *192.168.90.0/24* subnet:

```
/ip service
set api,api-ssl disabled=no address=192.168.90.0/24
```

Your organization's security requirements will dictate whether you use the API or API-SSL service. To be safe I would use API-SSL whenever possible.

FTP Controls

FTP shouldn't be used in production networks when SSH is a viable alternative. Sniffing cleartext FTP credentials off a network is trivially easy with freely-available software. As a stop-gap measure some servers support extensions of FTP that use TLS or SSL for encryption. Unfortunately, as of this writing RouterOS doesn't support FTP over TLS as shown in the FileZilla client's FTP login dialog in Figure 2.28:

```
Status: Connection established, waiting for welcome message
    ...
Status: Insecure server, it does not support FTP over TLS.
Status: Server does not support non-ASCII characters.
Status: Logged in
Status: Retrieving directory listing...
Status: Directory listing of "/" successful
```

Figure 2.28: Insecure FTP Server

If you're required to use FTP instead of SSH for file transfers there are some safeguards that can be put in place. Restricting file transfers to a specific host or management network is the most common control put around FTP. Restrict access to the *192.168.90.0/24* management network with the following command:

```
/ip service
set ftp address=192.168.90.0/24
```

While "security by obscurity" is never a valid control I would say it's not a bad idea to add a different port number for FTP to the control we just put in place:

```
/ip service
set ftp port=9999
```

> ⚠ **WARNING**: I've seen many customers trying to evade FTP port scans by changing port 20 and 21 to 2020 and 2121 respectively. This is a well-known tactic that won't fool attackers.

Winbox

Connections to the Winbox service are encrypted and secure by default. Even with secure connections we shouldn't be allowing just anyone to connect to our devices. Protecting access with robust credentials (p. 65) and using address restrictions creates another layer in the defense-in-depth strategy. Restrict Winbox access to management subnets *192.168.90.0/24* and *172.16.10.0/24* with the following commands:

```
/ip service
set winbox address=192.168.90.0/24,172.16.10.0/24
```

The *192.168.90.0/24* subnet has been referenced before but *172.16.10.0/24* hasn't. The latter could be a VPN subnet for remote administrators working from home or another helpdesk group in a remote network that's been integrated with the *192.168.0.0/16* infrastructure.

> **NOTE**: While Winbox connections are restricted by IP in this section MAC Winbox connections are still possible.

SNMP Configuration

Simple Network Management Protocol (SNMP) polls your devices for performance metrics and other data but it can also be leveraged by attackers. SNMP data from a router can include IP addresses, hostnames, location and contact information, model and vendor data, and more. An attacker that leverages SNMP for reconnaissance has a wealth of data at their fingertips. While SNMP can be used to read data from a device it can also be used to push configuration changes as well.

Create SNMP Community

If you want to use SNMP to monitor your devices the first step is creating a unique Community string. Use the following command to create a "*not_manito_networks*" Community string with *read-only permissions*:

```
/snmp community
add name="hey-manito" write-access=no read-access=yes
   addresses=192.168.88.10 security=authorized authentication
   -protocol=sha1 authentication-password="abc123!"
```

The "*addresses=192.168.88.10*" option stops any host from using the community that isn't 192.168.88.10. The equivalent configuration in Winbox is shown in Figure 2.29:

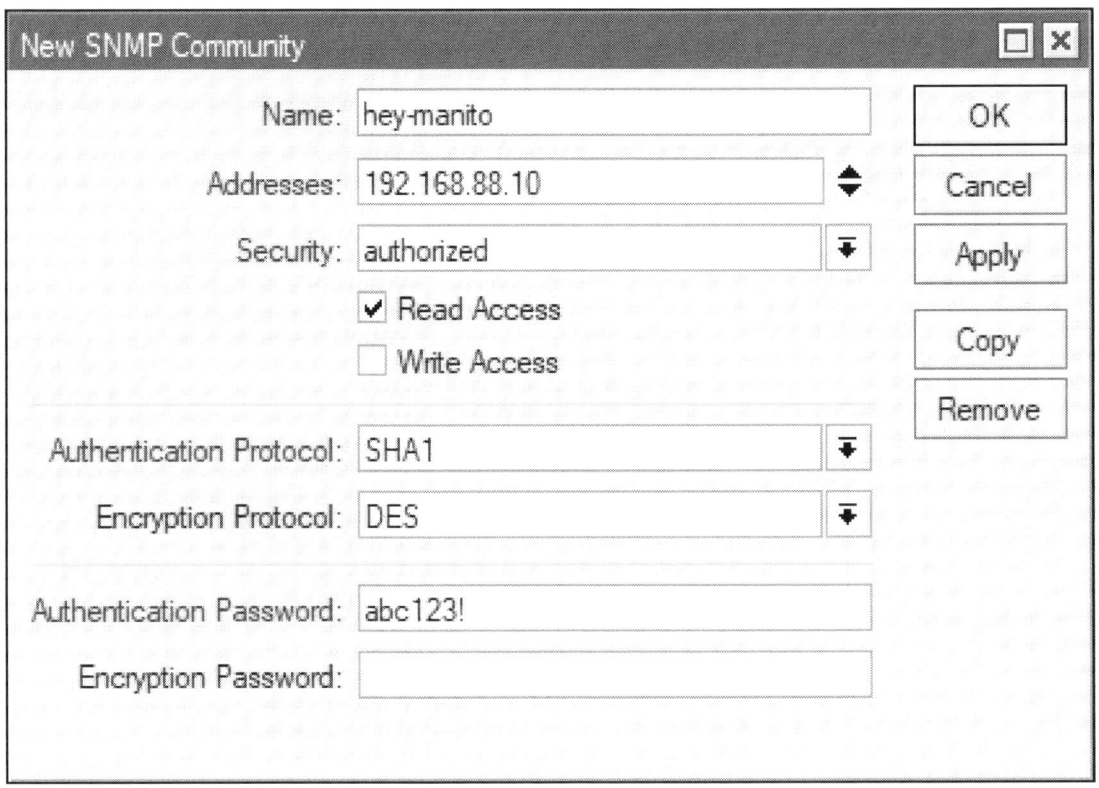

Figure 2.29: Winbox New SNMP Community

We'll use this more robust SNMP community on page 102 for network monitoring.

Secure Default Community

The default "*public*" community string can't be disabled or removed in RouterOS, either from Winbox or the CLI. Figure 2.30 on the following page shows the error given in Winbox when attempting to remove the default community:

Figure 2.30: Cannot Remove Default Community

Attackers doing reconnaissance on networks will typically try the "public" string, and I always like trying the company's name as well when I'm probing a client's network. Since the default Community string can't be removed or disabled we must rename it to something else an attacker won't know. Rename the string and remove its permissions with the following command:

```
/snmp community
set [find name=public] name=blah read-access=no write-access=
   no
```

SNMP Default Information

Now that SNMP is more secure we can enable it and set device information using the following commands:

```
/snmp
set enabled=yes
set contact="Tyler Hart" location="Main Street, USA"
```

Figure 2.31 on the next page shows the same information in the Winbox dialog:

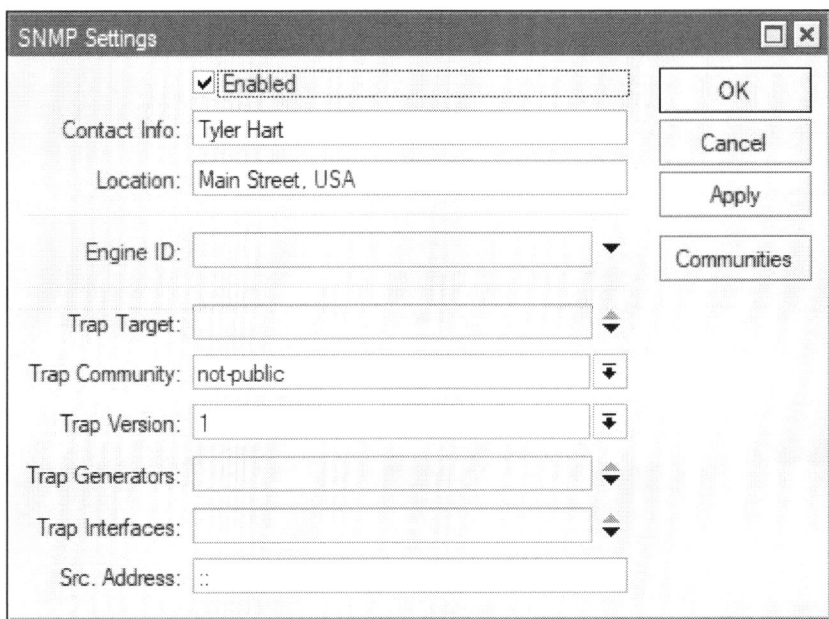

Figure 2.31: Typical SNMP Information

The contact name, location information, and hostname all come together to make a device easy to locate quickly in case you need to respond to an outage or security situation.

Universal Plug and Play

The UPnP service makes provisioning connectivity for devices that require port forwarding more straightforward. Unfortunately, the RouterOS implementation of UPnP offers little in the way of security controls around UPnP. If your organization isn't using UPnP at all use the following command to verify the service is disabled:

```
[admin@MikroTik] > /ip upnp print
                 enabled: no
allow-disable-external-interface: no
          show-dummy-rule: yes
[admin@MikroTik] > _
```

Figure 2.32: UPnP Default Configuration

If the UPnP service is in active use it's important to set the right *internal* and *external* interfaces. Only interfaces with hosts attached that need UPnP should have access to the service. The following commands would allow *vlan139*–connected hosts to use UPnP with *eth1* set as the external WAN port:

```
/ip upnp
set enabled=yes allow-disable-external-interface=no
```

```
interfaces set interface=ether1 type=external
interfaces set interface=vlan139 type=internal
```

Since the RouterOS implementation doesn't allow UPnP filtering by host address it's important to prune access by interface as much as possible.

SOCKS Proxy

The SOCKS service proxies TCP connections from one host to another. While there are practical uses of SOCKS proxying it's often used to circumvent network and application filtering. RouterOS has a SOCKS proxy service built-in and it's disabled by default. Ensure the SOCKS proxy is disabled with the command shown in Figure 2.33:

```
[admin@MikroTik] > /ip socks print
             enabled: no
                port: 1080
connection-idle-timeout: 2m
     max-connections: 200
[admin@MikroTik] > _
```

Figure 2.33: Default SOCKS Proxy Status

If the SOCKS service has been enabled use the "*/ip socks access print*" command and verify that all entries can be accounted for and are still in use.

Dynamic DNS Service

MikroTik provides a built-in dynamic DNS service for those who don't have a static Internet Protocol (IP) address but still want to access their devices via a domain name. This service can also update device time via MikroTik's cloud systems. This service may not present a threat but disabling features not in use or those that "phone home" to the manufacturer is required by many compliance standards. If you're not using the dynamic DNS capability turn it off with the following commands:

```
/ip cloud set ddns-enabled=no update-time=no
```

Chapter 3

Segmentation with VLANs

Segmenting networks for security is required for Payment Card Industry - Data Security Standard (PCI-DSS), Health Insurance Portability and Accountability Act (HIPAA), and other compliance standards. It's also considered an industry best practice, and it can isolate network failures to a single enclave. Using VLANs to logically separate a single physical network is often the easiest and most cost-effective way of splitting up networks for security. We'll do the following:

1. Determine what VLANs there should be
2. Create VLANs on the router
3. Assign IP addresses to the virtual VLAN interfaces
4. Configure an 802.1Q uplink on a switch
5. Firewall the VLANs as necessary

Having networks segmented logically also helps keep some measure of order and sanity in large network infrastructures.

VLAN Design

The first step in segmenting the networking isn't done on the router at all. Deciding how to structure your VLANs is typically done on a whiteboard with input from IT and organizational stakeholders. If a network is required to be HIPAA or PCI-DSS compliant this task is easier because it's spelled out in black and white what networks must be segmented. If network segmentation is happening for another reason, like a company mandate to improve security, then it's a bit "up in the air" but still doesn't have to be hard.

A typical VLAN topology will look something like the network in Figure 3.1 on the next page:

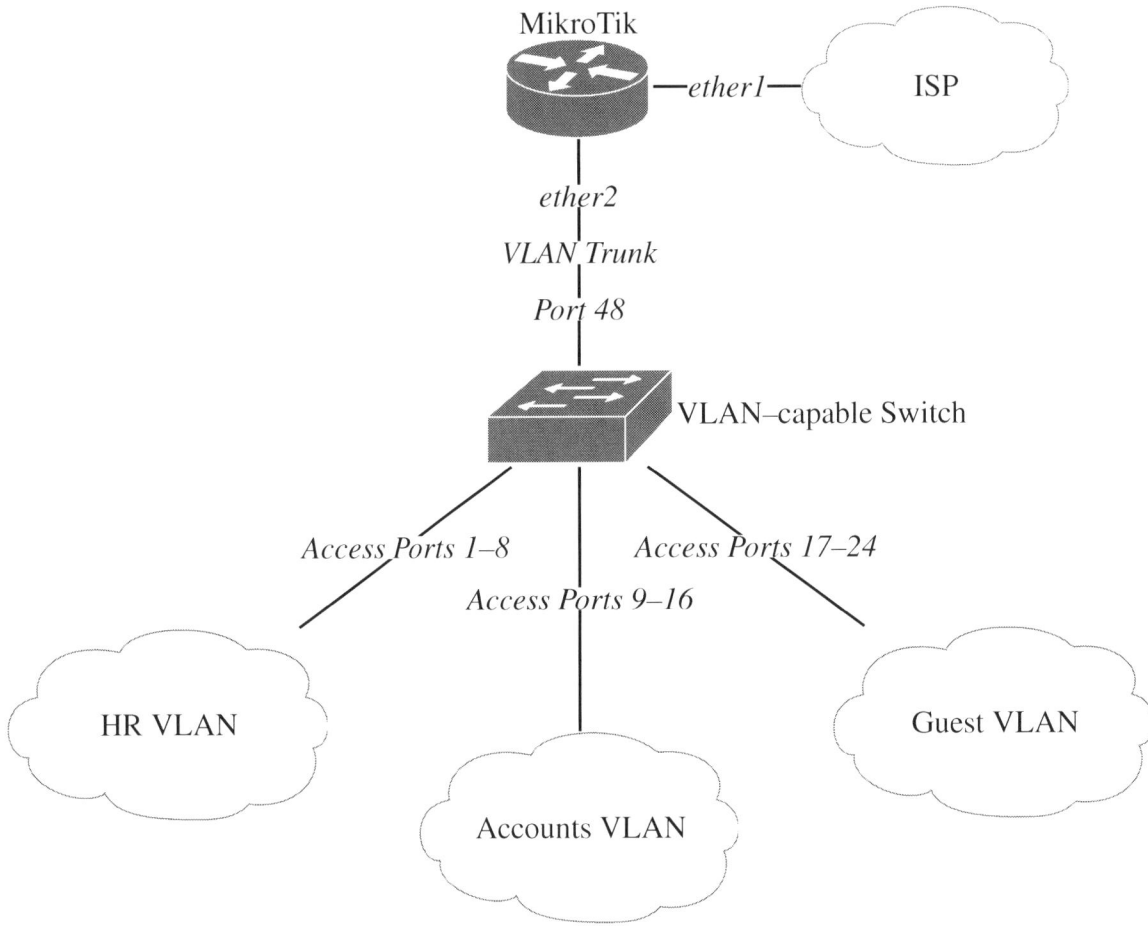

Figure 3.1: Typical VLAN Topology

For the most part I like to mirror the organizational structure with VLANs. Every department gets its own VLAN because each is its own logical group with unique functions. It's also easier to accommodate each department's security needs when they are split-out from the others. Servers and storage get their own VLANs, or (preferably) their own switching hardware if that's within budget. Building a separate storage network is especially important when using shared iSCSI resources. While a VLAN can work for iSCSI traffic it's always better to implement a separate storage network.

It's also helpful being able to monitor traffic per-department on their virtual interfaces. Tools like Torch or NetFlow can be used on each VLAN with only the traffic from a particular enclave being observed. Guest networks get their own VLANs that are firewalled from accessing the internal network. Wireless networks get their own VLANs too which keeps wireless "chatter", Apple iOS or Google Android updates, and push notification traffic off other networks. Once you decide who gets their own VLAN it's time to create them and segment the network.

Creating VLANs

First, create the VLANs on the MikroTik router and assign them to an interface with an uplink to a switch (e.g. *ether2*). Doing this step will automatically set 802.1Q trunking on the *ether2* interface and will take down the link for normal untagged traffic.

> ⚠ **WARNING**: This will create an outage until the rest of the steps are complete. You must also configure VLANs and trunking on your switches as necessary.

```
/interface vlan
add interface=ether2 name=HR vlan-id=100
add interface=ether2 name=Accounts vlan-id=150
add interface=ether2 name=Guests vlan-id=175

set HR comment="Human Resources"
set Accounts comment="Account Managers"
set Guests comment="Guest network access"
```

> **NOTE**: I've split out the commands for creating and commenting the interfaces so they don't wrap around the page multiple times. This is strictly for readability and doesn't affect system performance.

As mentioned earlier, creating the VLANs and assigning them to the physical ether2 interface automatically changes interface encapsulation to 802.1Q even though you won't see it in the interface details.

Addressing VLAN Interfaces

Next, we'll put IP addresses on the VLAN interfaces so they can function as gateways for their respective logical networks:

```
/ip address
add address=192.168.100.1/24 interface=HR
add address=192.168.150.1/24 interface=Accounts
add address=192.168.175.1/24 interface=Guests
```

I haven't set comments on the IP address entries because the VLAN interfaces have descriptive names and each already has a good comment. At this point we have our VLANs, and they have usable addresses. Now that the virtual networks have been created and assigned an IP address it's also possible to assign host addresses using Dynamic Host Configuration Protocol (DHCP).

Switch VLAN Configuration

The same VLANs will need to be created on the switches that will also be carrying traffic for those same virtual networks. Once VLANs have been created then access ports can be assigned for the hosts connecting to each VLAN. Perform the following steps on your switches:

1. Create VLANs
    - Use the same numerical VLAN ID - the name doesn't have to match but the numeric ID does
    - Give each VLAN a descriptive name
    - Set a useful description or remark for each VLAN
2. Assign switch uplink ports as "trunk" or "tagged" with your respective VLANs
3. Assign switch host ports as "access" or "untagged" for hosts in each VLAN

Every switch vendor has their own unique commands for accomplishing these steps. Consult your switch documentation before beginning VLAN configuration so you know what's required.

Firewalling VLANs

It's up to those doing network design and organizational stakeholders to decide what VLANs should be reachable by each network. Those rules are then implemented in the firewall. Since this traffic is being forwarded from one VLAN to another the rules would be placed on the firewall's *forward* chain (p. 48). Often hosts on one VLAN aren't allowed to communicate because they are members of separate, distinct groups. This type of isolation can limit the spread of a data breach or malware infection. Most often VLANs can send traffic out to the internet and to in-house servers like Active Directory Domain Controllers (DCs).

The following commands create a list of VLAN interfaces that will be referenced in firewall rules:

```
/interface list add name=VLANs

/interface list member
add interface=Accounts list=VLANs
add interface=Guest list=VLANs
add interface=HR list=VLANs
```

I've forgone adding a comment to the interface list because the name is descriptive enough. If we were creating multiple VLAN-oriented lists then it would be a good idea to add comments. Since hosts in the VLAN need to communicate with the internet we'll create a filter rule allowing traffic outbound on *ether1*. Reference the interface list created previously in the following command:

```
/ip firewall filter
add chain=forward in-interface-list=VLANs out-interface=
   ether1
```

While all VLANs share the same physical trunk line between the switch and router in Figure 3.1 on page 40 they will only be allowed to send traffic out *ether1* to the Internet Service Provider (ISP). The 802.1Q trunking protocol ensures that VLAN traffic remains segregated, even as it traverses the single trunk line.

Chapter 4

Firewalls

Firewalls filter traffic that is undesirable and allow authorized traffic into and across your networks. We can block port scanners and reconnaissance attempts, stop devices being co-opted into DDoS attacks, troubleshoot connectivity, and gather traffic statistics with the right rules. To leverage firewalls to protect your networks you must understand the following:

1. General best practices
2. Chains
3. Rules
4. Actions
5. States

The RouterOS firewall implementation is very closely related to the Linux *iptables* firewall. Both use much of the same technology and terminology but RouterOS brings additional features and management functionality. The sections in this chapter walk you through each component of the firewall.

Best Practices

To keep your networks secure and firewall rules from becoming too complicated there are some guidelines to follow. Consider your network operations in the context of these best practices:

- Allow traffic you need and block everything else
- Consolidate rules if possible for simplicity
- Sort rules for efficiency with the most-matched rules near the top
- Block all traffic at the end of each chain with final "catch-all" rules

- Periodically audit firewall configurations for consistency, efficiency, and security

Remember these best practices while learning more about the mechanics of firewalls in RouterOS.

Firewall Components

The RouterOS firewall uses three components to police traffic as it enters, leaves, or is forwarded across networks:

- Chains
- Rules
- Actions

Chains are mechanisms that process network traffic at different stages in the routing and bridging processes. Each chain has groups of rules applied that filter traffic depending on source, destination, and direction. Rules have actions assigned that affect whatever traffic is matched and apply an action (e.g. *drop*, *log*, *accept*). It's important to really understand each of these components when you're reading the following sections because they all work together. A great firewall rule with the right actions and the best comment to document it won't do you any good if it's applied to the wrong chain.

The packet flow documentation provided by MikroTik, shown in Figure 4.1, details the flow of packets through different interfaces and chains.

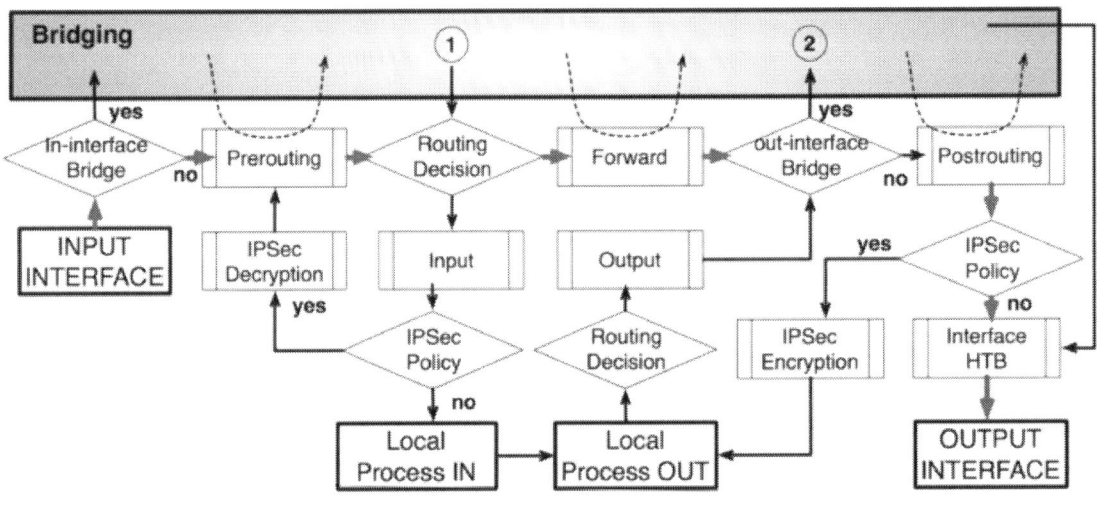

Credit: *MikroTik*

Figure 4.1: Routing Packet Flow

Firewall Chains

Three chains exist by default and cannot be removed:

- Input
- Forward
- Output

You can also create your own chains for more advanced firewalling and traffic monitoring. Each chain is a group of rules that processes a certain kind of traffic.

Input Chain

The input chain processes packets inbound to the router itself. An example of input traffic would be an administrator pinging a router's interface. Another example would be a Winbox session to a router. A diagram of output traffic is shown in Figure 4.2.

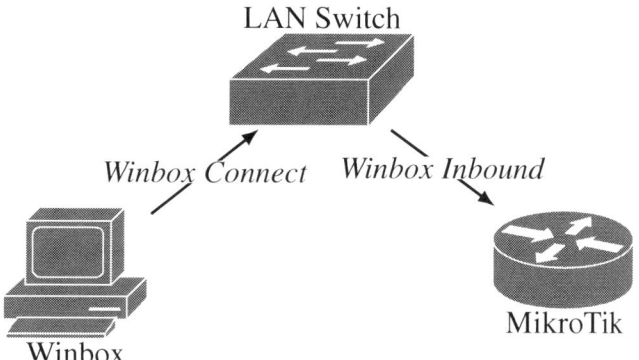

Figure 4.2: Input Chain Traffic

List all firewall Input chain rules with the following command:

```
/ip firewall filter print where chain=input
```

Input-type traffic should be blocked on outside connections like ISP uplinks because port scanners are constantly looking for open ports and running services[1]. Router access via services like SSH and Winbox should be allowed only from trusted subnets. With these services isolated network administrators have the opportunity to access device configurations and no one else.

---

[1] Both HIPAA and PCI-DSS compliance standards require that direct connections to the router be filtered.

Forward Chain

The forward chain processes packets passing through the router. An example of forward traffic would be a web browsing session that begins on a local network host and passes through the router headed toward a web server on the internet. Figure 4.3 shows an example of this type of traffic:

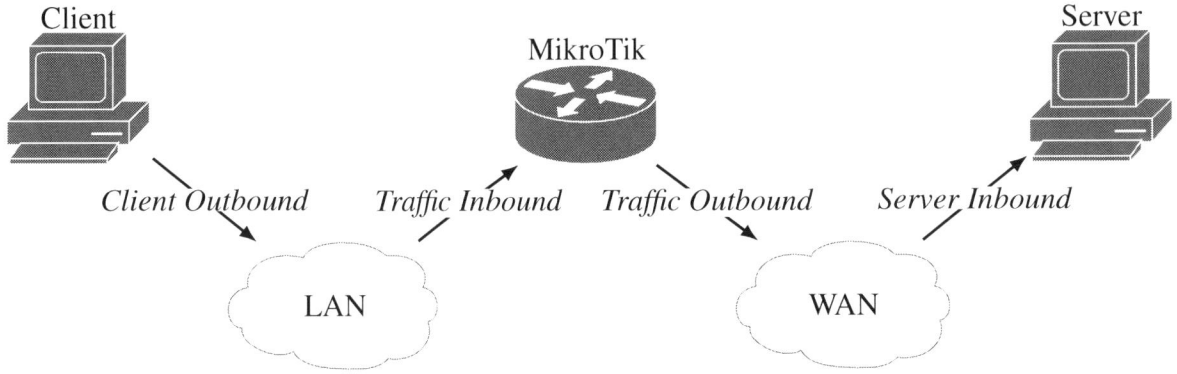

Figure 4.3: Forward Chain Traffic

This is *routed traffic* that the device is handing off from one network to another. Traffic isn't destined specifically for the router itself which means the input chain does not apply. As traffic leaves the router it isn't originating from RouterOS itself so output doesn't apply either. The majority of traffic being processed matches the forward chain on most routers. List all filter rules in the forward chain with the following command:

```
/ip firewall filter print where chain=forward
```

Output Chain

The Output chain processes traffic sent from the router. An example of traffic that matches the Output chain is a ping sent directly from the router's console. An Open Shortest Path First (OSPF) *hello* packet sent to another router or a Syslog message would also match the Output chain because it was sent from the router. A diagram of output traffic is shown in Figure 4.4 on the following page.

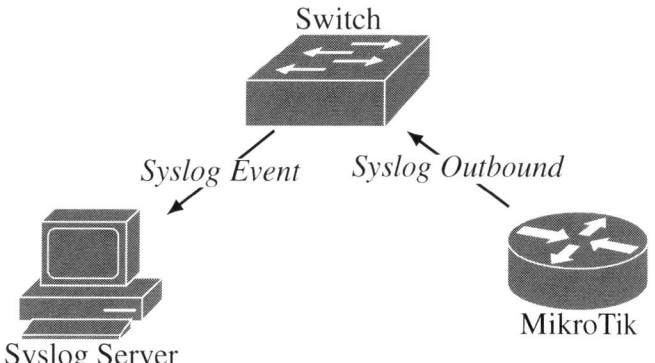

Figure 4.4: Output Chain Traffic

List all firewall Output chain rules with the following command:

```
/ip firewall filter print where chain=output
```

> **NOTE**: Many administrators don't apply much filtering to the Output chain because traffic originating from a router (like OSPF advertisements) is considered trusted.

Custom Chains

Custom chains are easily created to serve more specialized firewall needs. The following command creates a custom chain called "*ospf*":

```
/ip firewall filter
add chain=ospf comment="OSPF Chain"
```

We can put any rules built for OSPF into this chain to keep things organized and easier to understand. On page 59 we put this chain to work, processing traffic with separate rules.

Firewall Rules

Each rule entry in the firewall tells RouterOS what to do with matching packets. Firewall rules are applied to a chain and contain the criteria for matching packets. If a packet matches the criteria in a rule then the rule's action is applied. RouterOS allows for very flexible rules driven by many available criteria. The following are selections of typical criteria used for rules:

- Protocol
- Source Address
- Destination Address

- Source Port
- Destination Port
- Interface In
- Interface Out
- Internet Control Message Protocol (ICMP) Options
- Transmission Control Protocol (TCP) Flags
- Connection State

There are dozens of other criteria and any number of combinations for matching traffic that you're targeting with a rule.

Rule Evaluation

Firewall rules are evaluated in a top-down fashion. This means the firewall evaluates packets against rules starting at the top of a chain and moves down until a rule is matched or there are no more rules. If no rule matches traffic in the chain then the traffic is automatically allowed. For this reason, it's critical to have a final "catch-all" drop rule at the end of each chain.

Rule Sorting

There are a small handful of rules that match most traffic through any given chain in a typical network. Once identified those rules can be moved higher up the chain to eliminate wasteful processing of rules that don't get many matching packets. It's easy to see which rules these are by using the following commands:

```
/ip firewall filter
print stats chain=input
print stats chain=forward
print stats chain=output
```

Figure 4.5 on the following page shows default *forward* chain rules with IPSEC entries (1 and 2) that aren't in use being processed before rules (3 and 4) that match most of the traffic:

```
[admin@MikroTik] > /ip firewall filter print stats where
   chain=forward
Flags: X - disabled, I - invalid, D - dynamic
 #   CHAIN          ACTION                 BYTES         PACKETS
 0 D ;;; special dummy rule to show fasttrack counters
     forward        passthrough            13 031 576    17 961
 1   ;;; defconf: accept in ipsec policy
     forward        accept                 0             0
 2   ;;; defconf: accept out ipsec policy
     forward        accept                 0             0
 3   ;;; defconf: fasttrack
     forward        fasttrack-connection   958 977       5 727
 4   ;;; defconf: accept established,related, untracked
     forward        accept                 958 977       5 727
 5   ;;; defconf: drop invalid
     forward        drop                   0             0
 6   ;;; defconf:  drop all from WAN not DSTNATed
     forward        drop                   0             0
[admin@MikroTik] > _
```

Figure 4.5: Forward Chain Rule Order

Since IPSEC isn't used in this network the best option would be to remove rules one and two. If IPSEC were in use but not handling the bulk of network traffic the best option would be to move rules three and four above one and two. Once moved they will match the majority of traffic first, stopping the router from having to process other rules needlessly. For high-traffic networks this kind of sorting can result in huge processing overhead reductions.

Default Firewall Rules

The default firewall filter rules do a good job of protecting typical networks from outside attackers. While these rules can't protect against DDoS attacks they will deter in-depth port scans, remote authentication attempts, and more. The default rules are broken down by Chain and described in the following sections.

Input Chain Defaults

Figure 4.6 on the next page shows the default input chain filter rules:

```
[admin@MikroTik] > /ip firewall filter print where chain=
    input
Flags: X - disabled, I - invalid, D - dynamic
 0    ;;; defconf: accept established,related,untracked
 chain=input action=accept connection-state=established,
    related,untracked

 1    ;;; defconf: drop invalid
 chain=input action=drop connection-state=invalid

 2    ;;; defconf: accept ICMP
 chain=input action=accept protocol=icmp

 3    ;;; defconf: drop all not coming from LAN
 chain=input action=drop in-interface-list=!LAN
[admin@MikroTik] >
```

Figure 4.6: Default Input Chain Rules

A couple of the entries will need to be updated in high-security environments. The following list explains each input rule:

- Rule 1: *Invalid* connections headed inbound to the router are dropped in this rule. This can be spoofed or port scan traffic.

- Rule 2: ICMP traffic inbound to the router is allowed by this rule. Many technicians leave this rule in place for remote troubleshooting purposes. In organizations beholden to HIPAA or PCI-DSS this kind of unfiltered ICMP connection from any network or host isn't allowed.

- Rule 3: All remaining input traffic not originating from the LAN is dropped. In organizations with higher security requirements input traffic that isn't allowed by another rule would be dropped on *all* interfaces. This protects from external and internal threats.

Forward Chain Defaults

Figure 4.7 on the following page shows the default forward chain filter rules:

```
[admin@MikroTik] > /ip firewall filter print where chain=
   forward
Flags: X - disabled, I - invalid, D - dynamic
 0  D ;;; special dummy rule to show fasttrack counters
chain=forward action=passthrough

 1     ;;; defconf: accept in ipsec policy
chain=forward action=accept ipsec-policy=in,ipsec

 2     ;;; defconf: accept out ipsec policy
chain=forward action=accept ipsec-policy=out,ipsec

 3     ;;; defconf: fasttrack
chain=forward action=fasttrack-connection connection-state=
   established,related

 4     ;;; defconf: accept established,related, untracked
chain=forward action=accept connection-state=established,
   related,untracked

 5     ;;; defconf: drop invalid
chain=forward action=drop connection-state=invalid

 6     ;;; defconf:  drop all from WAN not DSTNATed
chain=forward action=drop connection-state=new connection-nat
   -state=!dstnat in-interface-list=WAN
[admin@MikroTik] >
```

Figure 4.7: Default Forward Chain Rules

These rules work in combination to expedite authorized traffic through the firewall while filtering spoofed and non-Network Address Translation (NAT) traffic from the outside. The following list explains each forward rule:

- Rule 0: This is a built-in dynamic rule that can't be removed. It shows how many packets have taken advantage of the FastTrack feature.

- Rules 1 and 2: Allows Internet Protocol Security (IPSEC) traffic through the firewall from local and remote networks. These rules aren't required if you're not using IPSEC Virtual Private Networks (VPNs).

- Rule 3: All traffic that is *established* or *related* has the *fasttrack-connection* applied. This action is covered on page 58.

- Rule 4: This rule allows all traffic that is *established* or *related*. It works with Rule number 3 to lower the resource utilization in the firewall for packets already allowed.

- Rule 5: Any *invalid* traffic being forwarded into or out of networks attached to the router are dropped. Ideally very little or no traffic at all should be matching this rule.

- Rule 6: The final rule drops all traffic being forwarded into or out of Wide Area Network (WAN) interfaces that has not been through the NAT process. This is typically a good rule in most organizations that NAT traffic through a single public IP assigned by their ISP.

Output Chain Defaults

Figure 4.8 shows there are no default output chain filter rules applied as of this writing:

```
[admin@MikroTik] > /ip firewall filter print where chain=
   output
Flags: X - disabled, I - invalid, D - dynamic

[admin@MikroTik] > _
```

Figure 4.8: Default Output Chain Rules

For most organizations this lack of output filtering won't affect network operation or security. We can add rules in this chain if we're curious about traffic patterns or volume, or to help troubleshooting. The following rule with the *accept* action simply passes OSPF traffic and increment packet and byte counters:

```
/ip firewall filter
add chain=output protocol=ospf action=accept comment="OSPF
   traffic counters"
```

This gives us an idea of the volume of OSPF traffic leaving the router.

Connection Tracking

RouterOS firewalls are *stateful*, meaning they track packets as part of an overall stream or connection. Packet traffic in an active connection that matches a firewall rule allowing traffic will be permitted. Once a connection's initial packets pass through the firewall the following traffic isn't checked because it's part of the same connection. Keeping track of connections and state allows for big boosts in efficiency. Packets that aren't part of an active connection but have spoofed sequence numbers are dropped or rejected. This connection tracking capability is critical to robust and efficient network isolation.

Connection States

Every packet is part of a connection, whether that connection has only a few packets or millions. All connections exist in one of four possible states:

1. New
2. Established
3. Related
4. Invalid

Firewall rules can be built around these connection states to filter traffic efficiently and log suspicious traffic.

New Connections

The first packet observed by the firewall in a stream of packets will be marked as *New*. This packet will be evaluated by firewall rules, and if it is allowed then the next packet going the other direction in that stream will create an *Established* connection.

Established Connections

A stream of network traffic that successfully passes packets both directions through the firewall is considered *Established*. Further packets in that connection will not be evaluated by the firewall because the first packets through were already allowed. Additional checking of the packets by the firewall would simply be a waste of resources since traffic going both directions in the connection was already checked against firewall rules.

Related Connections

Packets that are marked *Related* aren't part of a connection itself but they are related to one. An example mentioned in MikroTik's documentation[2] is an ICMP packet notifying the sender of an error in a connection. Protocols like FTP that use multiple ports can generate *Related* traffic. Point-to-Point Tunnel Protocol (PPTP) is another good example, with the connection using both TCP port 1723 and the Generic Route Encapsulation (GRE) protocol. Having a firewall entry that allows *Related* traffic cuts down on unnecessary rules.

---
[2]https://wiki.mikrotik.com/wiki/Manual:IP/Firewall/Filter#Properties

Invalid Connections

Network traffic that creates *Invalid* connections should almost always be dropped in the firewall. These types of packets could arrive at the router out-of-order or with an invalid sequence number. In production networks attached to the internet I often find *Invalid* connections are created by port scanners looking for open services. A router under extreme utilization that's dropping packets could also see traffic as *Invalid* because connections aren't able to properly initiate. The following command adds a firewall filter rule on the input chain that logs invalid connection attempts:

```
/ip firewall filter
add chain=input connection-state=invalid action=log log=yes
    log-prefix="Invalid connection"
```

Figure 4.9 shows logged results from a port scan in progress:

```
[admin@MikroTik] > /log print where message~"^Invalid
    connection"
sep/30 23:39:51 firewall,info Invalid connection input: in:
    bridge out:(unknown 0), src-mac e8:4e:06:43:fd:6b, proto
    TCP (RST), 192.168.1.77:39343->192.168.88.1:22, len 40
...
[admin@MikroTik] > _
```

Figure 4.9: Invalid Connections

From the logs I can see that the router at 192.168.88.1 received an RST-type TCP packet on port 22. RST-type packets headed to 192.168.88.1 from 192.168.1.77 aren't valid because there's no established session to reset. More than likely this port scan would be followed by login attempts over SSH using factory default and other well-known username and password combinations.

Comments

Adding comments to firewall rules as they are built is an important step that can save time in the future with minimal effort in the present. Having comments in place for rules also helps onboard new network administrators faster since they don't have to puzzle out what each rule is for. Most examples in this part of the book feature comments, even if they are just one word like on page 62. Comments should be descriptive - assume someone other than yourself is reading them as you're creating comments. They don't need to be overly-detailed but they should point a person who doesn't know the network intimately in the right direction.

> ⚠ **WARNING**: Avoid comments that require additional documentation to identify such as "Network 1", "Network 2", "Network 35", etc.

Firewall Actions

Firewall actions determine what the router does with packets that match a firewall rule. The main actions are discussed here, though there are others than enable more advanced traffic policing.

Accept

The *accept* action allows a packet through the firewall. The packet will not be processed by any further rules and continues to its destination. When accepting firewall traffic be sure to only accept traffic that is necessary - everything else should be dropped. The following command accepts ICMP traffic from a trusted network monitoring host at *192.168.88.10*:

```
/ip firewall filter
add chain=input protocol=icmp src-address=192.168.88.10
   action=accept comment="Network Monitoring"
```

Add to Address List

There are two address list-related actions and they both add an IP address to a list. The two individual actions are the following:

- *add-src-to-address-list*
- *add-dst-to-address-list*

One adds the Source (SRC) IP to a list, the other adds the Destination (DST) IP. The example command below adds the *source IP* of any telnet traffic (*TCP, port 23*) inbound to the WAN (*ether1*) to the "*Port Scanners*" address list. No production network should have Telnet open on the WAN interface, so any source IP of traffic matching this rule is probably a port scanner looking for soft targets. Create the rule with the following command:

```
/ip firewall filter
add chain=input protocol=tcp dst-port=23 in-interface=ether1
   action=add-src-to-address-list address-list="Port Scanners
"
```

It would be a good idea to add a timeout value to the *Port Scanners* address list so it doesn't balloon over time. The following firewall rule references that address list and blocks traffic inbound on *ether1*:

```
/ip firewall filter
chain=input action=drop in-interface=ether1 src-address-list
   ="Port Scanners" comment="Drop port scanners"
```

> **NOTE**: The *Drop* rule should be moved ABOVE the *add-src-to-address-list* rule so that IPs already on the list are blocked immediately, instead of being constantly re-added to the list.

Drop

The *drop* action forces the router to stop processing a packet. No further action is taken, and the traffic matching the rule is silently dropped. This is the preferred method for discarding unwanted traffic. It is considered a best practice to *accept* necessary traffic and *drop* everything else with a final rule at the end of each chain. The following rule drops all traffic that hasn't already been allowed and should be sorted to the end of the chain:

```
/ip firewall filter
add chain=input action=drop comment="DROP ALL"
```

> **NOTE**: This rule is effective as a "catch-all" because it has no criteria - it matches all protocols, all ports, all types of traffic.

FastTrack Connection

The *FastTrack* firewall action is special, and using it can have a tangible impact on your routers. Once a connection is FastTracked all future packets in the connection won't be checked against the firewall. If the first packet in a connection matches an *allow* rule there isn't any value in checking the packets that follow. For high-throughput devices or firewalls with a lot of rules not checking every single packet can save significant processing resources.

The default configuration for RouterOS firewalls is to FastTrack all connections that have a state of *established* or *related*. If a connection has already been established it's passed through the firewall successfully, so FastTracking the rest of the connection makes sense. The following two firewall rules work together to FastTrack connections:

```
/ip firewall filter
add chain=forward action=fasttrack-connection connection-
   state=established,related
```

```
add chain=forward action=accept connection-state=established,
    related
```

In a given packet stream, the first packet in a connection passes through the firewall successfully. This creates an *established* session in the connection table. The second packet of that established session to hit the firewall will match the first rule that has "*action=fasttrack-connection*" set. The rest of the packets in the connection will bypass the firewall from that point onward.

> **NOTE**: For best performance these rules should be placed at the top of the *forward* chain.

Jump

The *jump* action takes a packet being evaluated and moves it over to a different chain. Often this is used when custom chains have been built with special firewall rules. For example, the following rule takes any *input* chain traffic matching the *ospf protocol* and jumps it over to the *ospf chain* we already created on page 49.

```
/ip firewall filter
add protocol=ospf chain=input action=jump jump-target=ospf
```

The traffic will now be evaluated against rules in the custom *ospf* chain.

Log

The *log* action adds source and destination information for matching packets to the router's log. Traffic is passed on to the next firewall rule in the chain. As with the *passthrough* rules, it's recommended you disable or delete *log* rules when you're finished with them. Be aware that the log action could create a significant amount of log entries that fill up a device's storage and cause instability. The following command uses the *log* action to record inbound SSH traffic:

```
/ip firewall filter
add chain=input protocol=tcp dst-port=22 action=log
```

Figure 4.10 on the next page shows the result of the firewall rule's *log* action. Notice the log data that matches the firewall rule criteria (TCP protocol, port 22).

```
[admin@MikroTik] > /log print
16:23:55 firewall,info input: in:bridge out:(none), src-mac e8:4e:06:43:fd:6b, proto TCP (SYN), 192.168.1.40:9477->192.168.1.38:22,
    len 52
16:23:55 firewall,info input: in:bridge out:(none), src-mac e8:4e:06:43:fd:6b, proto TCP (ACK), 192.168.1.40:9477->192.168.1.38:22,
    len 40
16:23:55 firewall,info input: in:bridge out:(none), src-mac e8:4e:06:43:fd:6b, proto TCP (ACK,PSH),
    192.168.1.40:9477->192.168.1.38:22, len 68
16:23:55 firewall,info input: in:bridge out:(none), src-mac e8:4e:06:43:fd:6b, proto TCP (ACK,PSH),
    192.168.1.40:9477->192.168.1.38:22, len 712
16:23:55 firewall,info input: in:bridge out:(none), src-mac e8:4e:06:43:fd:6b, proto TCP (ACK,PSH),
    192.168.1.40:9477->192.168.1.38:22, len 64
16:23:55 firewall,info input: in:bridge out:(none), src-mac e8:4e:06:43:fd:6b, proto TCP (ACK,PSH),
    192.168.1.40:9477->192.168.1.38:22, len 312
...
16:24:17 system,error,critical login failure for user admin from 192.168.1.40 via ssh
16:24:17 system,info,account user admin logged in via local

[admin@MikroTik] > _
```

Figure 4.10: SSH Firewall Log

For troubleshooting you can also specify a *log-prefix* that adds custom text to the log message. This is useful for troubleshooting and easy to implement with the following command:

```
/ip firewall filter
add chain=input protocol=icmp action=log log-prefix="ICMP
    Traffic!"
```

NOTE: Move this filter rule above the final *drop* rule or it'll never log any traffic.

An example of log entries created by the rule are shown in Figure 4.11.

```
17:17:19 firewall,info ICMP Traffic! input: in:bridge out:(
    none), src-mac 74:c6:3b:64:05:89, proto ICMP (type 3, code
    3), 192.168.88.253->192.168.88.1, len 145
```

Figure 4.11: Logged ICMP Traffic

Passthrough

The *passthrough* action adds byte and packet counts to the rule's statistics then allows the traffic to continue being processed. This is helpful when determining if a certain kind of traffic is hitting your firewall. Disable or remove passthrough rules when you're done with them so as not to add processing overhead. The following command uses passthrough to get counter information for SSH traffic:

```
/ip firewall filter
add chain=input protocol=tcp dst-port=22 action=passthrough
```

View the statistics for all rules with the *passthrough* action:

```
/ip firewall filter
print stats where action=passthrough
```

Reject

The *reject* action forces the router to discard matching packets but doesn't do it silently like the drop action does. Instead an ICMP message is sent to notify the sender that traffic was dropped. This could allow an attacker running port scans to fingerprint your device and continue reconnaissance efforts. For this reason, the reject action is not the preferred method for discarding unwanted traffic. Some compliance standards like PCI-DSS and HIPAA specifically require that unwanted traffic be silently dropped, not discarded.

For testing purposes a firewall rule blocking all ICMP from *192.168.88.253* to the router was created and moved to the top of the input chain:

```
/ip firewall filter
chain=input action=reject protocol=icmp src-address
   =192.168.88.253
```

Figure 4.12 shows the result of an ICMP echo (*ping*) that matches the rule just created.

```
[admin@MikroTik] > ping 192.168.88.1
Pinging 192.168.88.1 with 32 bytes of data:

Reply from 192.168.88.1: Destination net unreachable.
[admin@MikroTik] > _
```

Figure 4.12: ICMP Reject Results

Note the "*Reply from 192.168.88.1 ...*" portion of the text response. The ICMP type three[3] message informs an attacker doing reconnaissance that a device is online with some kind of filtering. That attacker can now further tailor reconnaissance attempts to unmask the device. Figure 4.13 on the next page shows the result of that same rule and test *ping* but with the *drop* action instead of *reject*.

---

[3]https://www.iana.org/assignments/icmp-parameters/icmp-parameters.xhtml#icmp-parameters-types

```
[admin@MikroTik] > ping 192.168.88.1
Pinging 192.168.88.1 with 32 bytes of data:

Request timed out.
[admin@MikroTik] > _
```

Figure 4.13: ICMP Drop Results

This is what an attacker doing reconnaissance should see - nothing at all. The difference in results is why it's so important to understand the consequences of using *reject*.

Return

The *return* action sends traffic back to the chain that it was originally *jumped* from (p. 59). If you have a special chain set up for traffic analysis or troubleshooting you can *return* traffic to the original chain so it gets processed by the rest of its rules.

Tarpit

The *tarpit* action keeps TCP connections open and deliberately slows responses to traffic sources that match a firewall rule. These traffic sources could be port scanners, spammers, or other unsavory types. Some DDoS mitigation providers and large enterprises who deal with Distributed Denial of Service (DoS) (DDoS) attacks use tarpitting to slow them down. However, with botnets numbering in the thousands or tens–of–thousands this can have a limited effectiveness. Be aware that using tarpit keeps connections open so applying this action on a lot of traffic places significant load on a device.

Address Lists

Address lists help you consolidate and simplify firewall rules. They can also help with the network documentation process. Address lists are objects that firewall rules can reference made up of individual hosts or entire subnets. An example of a network topology that can use an address list is shown in Figure 4.14 on the following page.

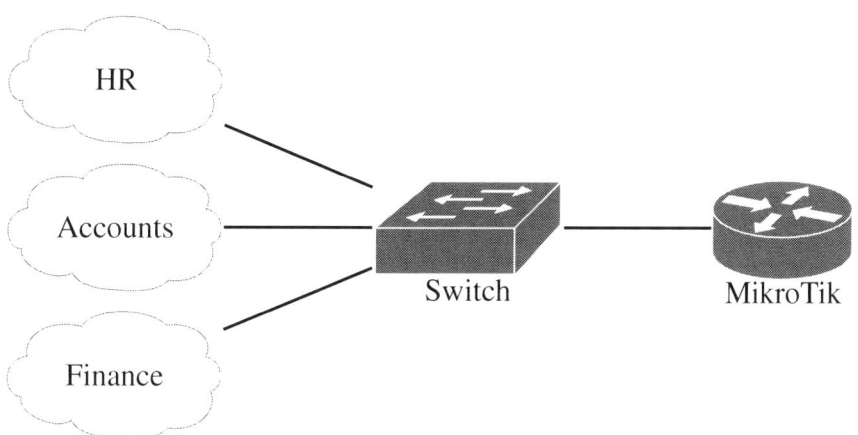

Figure 4.14: Address Group Topology

To create an address list just add an entry. If the list didn't exist before it will be created automatically. Deleting the final entry in an address list removes the list as well. The following command creates an address list containing three subnets, each one a local network behind a router:

```
/ip firewall address-list
add addr=192.168.1.0/24 list=LANs comment=HR
add addr=192.168.2.0/24 list=LANs comment=Accounts
add addr=192.168.3.0/24 list=LANs comment=Finance
```

Each network gets its own entry and comment but they are all part of the "Local Nets" list. Entries can be added or removed from Address Lists without changing the firewall rules that reference them. If a new network *192.168.4.0/24* was brought online a simple */ip firewall address-list add ...* command adds the network to the list and all firewall rules will automatically apply.

The following command uses the address list to allow traffic out *ether1* from all those networks:

```
/ip firewall filter
add chain=forward src-address-list=LANs out-interface=ether1
   action=accept comment="LANs to WAN"
```

What would have taken three total rules (one for each network) now is done in one rule. This solution scales well as your networks grow and firewalling becomes more complex. Sorting rules becomes easier as well, because just one rule needs to be moved up or down the firewall chain instead of three. This kind of simplicity also helps prevent human error (and downtime).

Chapter 5

User Credentials

Having the best firewall rules in the world and locking down IP services won't do us any good if the factory-default credentials are still in place. The default credentials are easily guessed and take less than a minute to find on the internet. Locking down credentials is a critical part of router security.

Default Admin Account

First, let's set a password on the default admin user, then change the admin username to something other than the factory default "admin". This is required per Infrastructure Router STIG Finding V-3143:

> "Network devices must not have any default manufacturer passwords."

Just like renaming the Administrator account on Microsoft Windows servers it's a good idea to rename the MikroTik admin user to something other than a known default *admin*:

```
/user
set admin password=abc123!
set admin name=tikadmin comment="BACKUP ONLY"
```

Additional Accounts

All router administrators should have their own logins for the purpose of non-repudiation, and only use those logins to administer the device. The default login that cannot be deleted should only be used for emergency login purposes. Using individual accounts is required per Infrastructure Router STIG Finding V-3056:

> "Group accounts must not be configured for use on the network device."

Create a user for each administrator accessing the device:

```
/user
add name=tyler password=abc123! group=full comment="Tyler
   Hart"
```

The *admin* user we just renamed should only be used for backup access purposes if other credentials somehow were lost or forgotten. This also allows quick disabling of an administrator's access when they leave the organization without affecting other administrative access.

For each user it's possible to restrict access only to a specific network using the following command:

```
/user set tyler address=192.168.90.0/24
```

This can work together with a time-based firewall *input* rule that only allows SSH or Winbox access from *192.168.90.0/24* to the device within pre-defined working hours. Any other access would have to be from a local console, restricting it to people with access to the device's physical location.

Adverse Accounts

When an administrator leaves the organization their access to the router should be removed so they are unable to change any configurations. If an administrator goes on a leave of absence or is put on some manner of "legal hold" it can also be a good idea to temporarily disable their access, depending on the company's compliance requirements and legal counsel input.

To disable an account, use the "*disable*" command:

```
/user disable [find name=tyler]
```

The "*enable*" command restores the users access to the device. To delete an account, use the "*remove*" command:

```
/user remove [find name=tyler]
```

Proactively managing accounts on your routers satisfies Infrastructure Router STIG Finding V-3058:

> "Unauthorized accounts must not be configured for access to the network device."

> **NOTE**: It's considered prudent in the industry to audit users on your infrastructure devices **at least** every six months. Disable or remove credentials that are no longer active or should no longer be in place. There are ways to automate this task via the API, or an orchestration system like Ansible.

Groups

User groups determine which permissions the group members have on a device. Three groups are configured by default:

- Full
- Read
- Write

Full Group

Members of the Full group can make configuration changes on the device, add and remove users, change packages, and all other tasks. Only users with network administration experience and a genuine organizational need should be granted Full group access. Examples of these types of users include the following:

- Senior network administrators
- Network administrators responsible for creating device credentials
- Technicians actively managing User Manager or Hotspot functionality

Read Group

The Read group allows its members to view device configurations and performance but not save changes. Network and security analysts, system administrators who need to see network service status, and others can safely have access via the Read group without worry they can change things.

- Network analysts responsible for basic troubleshooting and performance monitoring
- Network security analysts responsible for log monitoring
- Technicians or administrators performing network compliance scanning with Nessus, OpenVAS, etc.

Write Group

The Write group has the same permissions as the Full group except for the rights to log in via FTP, manage users, and work with The Dude. This group is appropriate for the following types of users:

- Network administrators who are responsible for maintaining and troubleshooting networks

- Experienced network analysts working with administrators

Custom Groups

The three default groups cannot be removed but you can create your own custom groups. Users can only be a member of one group so if the three default groups don't meet your security needs create a custom group with the necessary permissions. A custom group can be especially useful for new network administrators that should be able to make minimal changes and monitor devices but not perform tasks that could break a device's configuration.

The following commands create a custom group that allows a user to read non-sensitive configuration information, transfer files via FTP, and log in via Winbox for monitoring:

```
/user group
add name="Network Analysts" policy=winbox,ftp,read,!sensitive
```

The exclamation point in front of "*sensitive*" means "*not sensitive*". With this permission entry analysts can't see wireless or IPSEC keys, user manager credentials, etc. More experienced analysts could also be put in the same type of group that also has the "*reboot*" option added if the organization is comfortable with them being able to reboot devices.

Custom groups are also useful if your organization brings outside MikroTik consultants into the network to perform engineering or security tasks. Using a custom group would allow the consultants to make changes to the network but not view sensitive keys or reboot the device. This would force the outside party to work with your internal staff to access sensitive information or reboot devices and create an outage.

Active Users

To view users currently logged in to a device use the "*/user active print*" command. For a list of users currently logged in, their source IP, login service and time, and user group use the "*detail*" option shown in Figure 5.1 on the following page.

```
[admin@MikroTik] > /user active print detail
Flags: R - radius, M - by-romon
 0  when=sep/23/2017 15:59:13 name="tyler" address=74:C6:3B
    :64:05:89 via=winbox group=full

 1  when=sep/23/2017 16:00:48 name="tyler" via=console group=
    full

 2  when=sep/23/2017 16:02:45 name="tyler" address
    =192.168.1.43 via=ssh group=full

[admin@MikroTik] > _
```

Figure 5.1: Printing Active Users

The output of this command is very unusual for a few reasons:

1. The same admin-level user "*tyler*" is logged in from multiple locations

2. The active user accessed the device using different protocols at the same time

3. The user is using both local and remote access simultaneously

In a production network this is a good indication that multiple people are using the same set of credentials which violates the *non-repudiation principle*. If an administrator's primary location is the same as the device this could also be a tell-tale sign of stolen credentials being used remotely as well. To see a record of which users logged in from where, when, and via which protocol use the command in Figure 5.2:

```
[admin@MikroTik] > /log print where message~"logged in from"
15:00:31 system,info,account user tyler logged in from 74:C6
    :3B:64:05:89 via winbox
15:07:50 system,info,account user tyler logged in from 74:C6
    :3B:64:05:89 via winbox
15:59:13 system,info,account user tyler logged in from 74:C6
    :3B:64:05:89 via winbox
16:00:30 system,info,account user tyler logged in from
    192.168.1.43 via ssh
16:00:44 system,info,account user tyler logged in from
    192.168.1.43 via telnet

[admin@MikroTik] > _
```

Figure 5.2: User Logged In Entries

Chapter 6

Centralizing AAA with RADIUS

Credential management can be especially difficult as the network scales and device count grows. Credentials need to be created, updated, disabled, and eventually deleted over the course of their lifetime. Credential usage also needs to be monitored and audited periodically. To be successful in securing the network it's important to understand all the components of the AAA framework:

- Authentication
- Authorization
- Accounting

Each of these components contributes to a defense-in-depth strategy and supports proper IT governance. We'll examine each part of the AAA framework in the following sections.

Authentication

Authentication happens when a system verifies a user or device is who they purport to be. FreeRADIUS can use credential information in the *users* file or a SQL database. The NPS role in Windows Server uses Active Directory credentials to authenticate RADIUS clients. It should be noted that successful authentication does not mean that a user or device will be allowed to make changes. An authenticated user or system simply is who they say that they are. The rights and permissions granted after successful authentication are applied via authorization processes.

Authorization

Once a user or device has been authenticated it is authorized to perform certain actions based on its permission levels. RouterOS relies on the RADIUS *group* attribute to determine what users can and cannot do on a MikroTik system. These groups were already discussed on page 67, and you can tailor your own groups as necessary. The changes made by an authenticated, authorized user are logged by an accounting system. This chapter relies on RADIUS to provide standardized accounting, and it is very well-suited to the task.

Accounting and Accountability

If a network breach is suspected the following information can be readily at-hand when systems are configured properly for accounting:

1. What credentials failed or succeeded in authenticating?
   - Are there any unrecognized accounts?
   - Are accounts being used assigned admin-level privileges?
2. Which devices were accessed?
   - Are these user-facing or infrastructure devices?
   - Are the devices being accessed part of a sensitive system?
3. What changes were made on these devices?
   - Accounts created or modified
   - Firewall filter rules changed or disabled
   - Ports forwarded from the outside to internal systems
4. When did these changes occur?
   - Were changes made inside or outside normal hours?
   - Do changes correspond with a scheduled outage or maintenance window?

Being able to make careful observations of all device activity and answer these questions means that network administrators and users can be held accountable for their actions.

Onboarding

As networks grow and device count increases it becomes harder to onboard new administrators. Past a certain point it becomes essential to centralize account management with a system like FreeRADIUS. When new administrators come onboard it's important to get them access to devices quickly so they can dive into the new network, start learning the lay of the land, and begin contributing. If your organization has 200 MikroTik devices and a new employee ("Tyler") you'd have to do this on every device:

```
/user add name=tyler password=abc123! group=full comment="
   Tyler Hart"
```

As your network grows the task of adding new users grows along with it.

Passwords

Changing passwords for each administrator on each device manually is cumbersome and difficult to do consistently every time. Again, if you had 200 devices and changed passwords for administrators every 90 days this would be required on every device:

```
/user set tyler password=abc123!
```

For 200 devices and passwords changing four times a year that's 800 of that command *per administrator*. That kind of overheard simply isn't sustainable long-term and may lead to administrators neglecting to update credentials regularly.

Offboarding

When an administrator resigns, is placed on legal hold or administrative leave, or is terminated it's important to immediately block network access. This protects the organization and customer data on the network. For 200 MikroTik devices and a disgruntled employee you'd have to do one of these 200 times (and quickly) once alerted by HR:

```
/user set tyler disabled=yes comment="LEGAL HOLD"
/user remove tyler
```

To do this quickly and consistently across hundreds of devices is difficult without some kind of centralization.

RADIUS and FreeRADIUS

The Remote Authentication Dial-In User Service (RADIUS) protocol is an open and well-supported AAA standard in the networking industry. Other proprietary protocols exist like TACACS+ that do AAA, but RADIUS is the dominant open standard. Many RADIUS servers exist, both commercial and open source, and for this guide we'll rely on a well-known open source solution FreeRADIUS. The Microsoft Windows NPS role can handle RADIUS requests, as can Cisco's ACS product. Open source solutions include FreeRADIUS and others, with additional libraries for managing and manipulating records.

FreeRADIUS Installation

We'll begin by installing FreeRADIUS on Ubuntu Linux. For this book I've used a basic Ubuntu Server 16.04 installation with no additional configuration or tools installed. First update APT repositories, then install FreeRADIUS with the following commands:

```
sudo apt-get update
sudo apt-get install freeradius
```

Enable the FreeRADIUS service so it starts when the system boots automatically. Then restart the service to ensure it's running before going further:

```
sudo systemctl enable freeradius
sudo systemctl restart freeradius
```

View the FreeRADIUS service status using the command shown in Figure 6.1:

```
admin@radius-server:~$ systemctl status freeradius
 freeradius.service - FreeRADIUS multi-protocol policy server
Loaded: loaded (/lib/systemd/system/freeradius.service;
   enabled; vendor preset: enabled)
Active: active (running) since Thu 2017-09-14 14:49:41 UTC;
   40s ago
Docs: man:radiusd(8)
man:radiusd.conf(5)
http://wiki.freeradius.org/
http://networkradius.com/doc/
...
```

Figure 6.1: FreeRADIUS Service Status

To view logs generated by the FreeRADIUS service you can use the *more* command on */var/log/freeradius/radius.log* as follows:

```
sudo more /var/log/freeradius/radius.log
```

```
admin@radius-server:~$ sudo more /var/log/freeradius/radius.
   log
[sudo] password for tyler: **********
Thu Sep 14 14:48:59 2017 : Info: Debugger not attached
Thu Sep 14 14:48:59 2017 : Warning: [/etc/freeradius/3.0/mods
   -config/attr_filter/access_reject]:11 Check item "
   FreeRADIUS-Response-Delay"     found in filter list for
   realm "DEFAULT".
Thu Sep 14 14:48:59 2017 : Warning: [/etc/freeradius/3.0/mods
   -config/attr_filter/access_reject]:11 Check item "
   FreeRADIUS-Response-Delay-USec"  found in filter list for
   realm "DEFAULT".
Thu Sep 14 14:48:59 2017 : Info: Loaded virtual server <
   default>
...
```

Figure 6.2: FreeRADIUS Log

Dictionary Files

FreeRADIUS uses dictionary files to map RADIUS fields for different vendors including MikroTik. The command in Figure 6.3 on the next page will list all the dictionary files in the */usr/share/freeradius* directory:

```
admin@radius-server:~$ ls -l /usr/share/freeradius/
total 1524
-rw-r--r-- 1 root root     8741 Jul 26 14:23 dictionary
-rw-r--r-- 1 root root     1499 Jul 26 14:23 dictionary.3com
-rw-r--r-- 1 root root     2346 Jul 26 14:23 dictionary.3gpp
-rw-r--r-- 1 root root     5414 Jul 26 14:23 dictionary.3gpp2
-rw-r--r-- 1 root root    10920 Jul 26 14:23 dictionary.acc
-rw-r--r-- 1 root root     9605 Jul 26 14:23 dictionary.acme
-rw-r--r-- 1 root root      425 Jul 26 14:23 dictionary.actelis
-rw-r--r-- 1 root root      366 Jul 26 14:23 dictionary.adtran
-rw-r--r-- 1 root root      631 Jul 26 14:23 dictionary.
   aerohive
-rw-r--r-- 1 root root      633 Jul 26 14:23 dictionary.
   airespace
-rw-r--r-- 1 root root     3652 Jul 26 14:23 dictionary.alcatel
...
```

Figure 6.3: FreeRADIUS Dictionary Files

Many online tutorials still include steps for adding fields by hand but modern releases of FreeRADIUS have a MikroTik dictionary file located in */usr/share/freeradius*. The *dictionary.mikrotik* file has all the fields you need to utilize MikroTik with FreeRADIUS. The *"more /usr/share/freeradius/dictionary.mikrotik"* command will list all the fields in the dictionary file. Figure 6.4 on the following page shows a selection of the fields in the dictionary file:

```
VENDOR              Mikrotik                             14988

BEGIN-VENDOR        Mikrotik

ATTRIBUTE           Mikrotik-Recv-Limit                  1
   integer
ATTRIBUTE           Mikrotik-Xmit-Limit                  2
   integer

# this attribute is unused
ATTRIBUTE           Mikrotik-Group                       3
   string

ATTRIBUTE           Mikrotik-Wireless-Forward            4
   integer
ATTRIBUTE           Mikrotik-Wireless-Skip-Dot1x         5
   integer
ATTRIBUTE           Mikrotik-Wireless-Enc-Algo           6
   integer
ATTRIBUTE           Mikrotik-Wireless-Enc-Key            7
   string
ATTRIBUTE           Mikrotik-Rate-Limit                  8
   string
ATTRIBUTE           Mikrotik-Realm                       9
   string
ATTRIBUTE           Mikrotik-Host-IP                     10
   ipaddr
ATTRIBUTE           Mikrotik-Mark-Id                     11
   string
ATTRIBUTE           Mikrotik-Advertise-URL               12
   string
ATTRIBUTE           Mikrotik-Advertise-Interval          13
   integer
...
```

Figure 6.4: MikroTik Dictionary File Attributes

The number *14988* on the first line is used on page 85 when creating a custom RADIUS attribute in the NPS role on Windows Server. Attribute number three, *Mikrotik-Group*, is also used to indicate what RouterOS group the authenticated user is a member of (full, read, write, or custom).

FreeRADIUS Logging

By default FreeRADIUS does not log authentication attempts, either successful or failed. It's important to log authentication attempts in case of stolen credentials or password guessing attempts. Modify the */etc/freeradius/radiusd.conf* file and change the *auth* option to *yes*. Some organizations like to log bad passwords so they can be observed, and the *auth_badpass* option shown below would allow you to do that. Use your favorite text editor to make changes to */etc/freeradius/3.0/radiusd.conf* so it reflects the following:

```
...
#   Log authentication requests to the log file.
#
#   allowed values: {no, yes}
#
auth = yes

#   Log passwords with the authentication requests.
#   auth_badpass  - logs password if it's rejected
#   auth_goodpass - logs password if it's correct
#
#   allowed values: {no, yes}
#
auth_badpass = no
auth_goodpass = no
...
```

If your organization operates honeypots to detect malicious activity using the *auth_badpass* option can help gather network intelligence about threats. In production environments it's not a good idea to log passwords using the *auth_badpass* or *auth_goodpass* options because it will save cleartext passwords in the log.

Configuration Files

All RADIUS clients and users are contained in either configuration files or a back-end database. Setting up and configuring a back-end database is beyond the scope of this guide, but the MikroTik configuration is the same. Default entries in the FreeRADIUS configuration files can be used to point it to a database vice the built-in configuration files.

Clients.conf File

The */etc/freeradius/clients.conf* file contains all the entries for RADIUS clients that are allowed to send AAA requests to the server. RADIUS clients aren't the users we are authenticating, but they are the devices that make authentication requests to RADIUS on your behalf. Only devices with entries in the file are allowed to use RADIUS so we'll configure that first. Use the *nano* command - or your favorite text editor - to edit the clients.conf file:

```
sudo nano /etc/freeradius/3.0/clients.conf
```

Add entries for every device that will use RADIUS for AAA:

```
client MikroTik-router {
    ipaddr = 192.168.88.1
    secret = abc123!
}
```

> **NOTE**: The *secret* for each device should be **complex and unique**.

Users File

The */etc/freeradius/users* file contains all the user credentials that can authenticate to our MikroTik devices via RADIUS. Modify the *users* file with *nano* or your favorite text editor:

```
sudo nano /etc/freeradius/3.0/users
```

Add a user with the following entry in the *users* file:

```
tyler    Cleartext-Password := "mikrotik"
         Group = "full"
```

There is a tab between *tyler* and the *Cleartext-Password...* attribute. Two tabs are entered before the start of the *Group = ...* attribute. Ensure that the username being created doesn't match one already on the Linux server itself. The ":=" symbols for the password isn't a typo. That combination is part of the formatting standard for the *users* file. If you don't want to store plaintext passwords in the *users* file you can use MD5 hashes instead. This certainly isn't perfect but it adds an additional layer of security.

First use the *md5sum* command as follows:

```
md5sum
[Type plaintext password, DO NOT hit <Enter>]
<Ctrl-D><Ctrl-D>
```

The hash can be carefully copied from the output of the *md5sum* command immediately after your password. Now we'll use *Crypt-Password* instead of the *Cleartext-Password* option and copy–paste the hash. We must also specify the *Auth-Type = digest* option to indicate we're using MD5 as follows:

```
tyler    Crypt-Password := "04482bf439e50529c375a9dffacb88b7"
         Auth-Type = digest
         Group = "full"
```

User Group

The *Group* option for each user in the */etc/freeradius/3.0/users* file maps directly to the user's Group in RouterOS. You can fine-tune user permissions by creating custom user groups and using those in the FreeRADIUS *user* configuration file. We're using the default *full* group for administrators, which is why *Group = "full"* is included in the file. Refer to page 67 for more information on creating groups. For information on what each group option gives a user permission to do see the MikroTik documentation at the following URL:

`https://wiki.mikrotik.com/wiki/Manual:Router_AAA#User_Groups`

Restart the FreeRADIUS service then check the status to verify there were no mistakes in the configuration files:

```
sudo systemctl restart freeradius
systemctl status freeradius
```

Windows Server 2016 RADIUS

The NPS role can run RADIUS on Microsoft Windows Server. This section is written to the 2016 version of Microsoft Windows Server since it's the most recent stable release. Implementing RADIUS authentication with NPS on Widows Server allows users to authenticate with their Active Directory credentials. This gives a true "single-sign-on" (SSO) experience across our MikroTik infrastructure. Unfortunately there is added complexity with this kind of integration.

We'll complete the following steps to enable RADIUS integration between RouterOS and Active Directory:

1. Evaluate licensing requirements (Windows)
2. Install and configure the NPS server role (Windows)
3. Grant users login rights in Active Directory (Windows)
4. Create MikroTik RADIUS clients (Windows)
5. Test and verify authentication (RouterOS)

Windows Server 2016 Licensing Requirements

Windows Server 2016 instances licensed with Standard Edition keys have some NPS limitations:

1. Maximum of 50 RADIUS clients total
2. Can't use address ranges to define groups of clients

Instances licensed with Datacenter Edition keys support an unlimited number of clients and they can be defined by address ranges. Your Microsoft licensing level and number of RADIUS clients will determine if RADIUS with NPS is an acceptable solution for your organization[1].

Installing and Configuring NPS

The NPS role is easily installed on Windows Server 2016 with PowerShell. Use the following command at an administrative PowerShell prompt:

```
install-windowsfeature -name npas
```

Reboot the server if necessary, then open the NPS management window as shown in Figure 6.5:

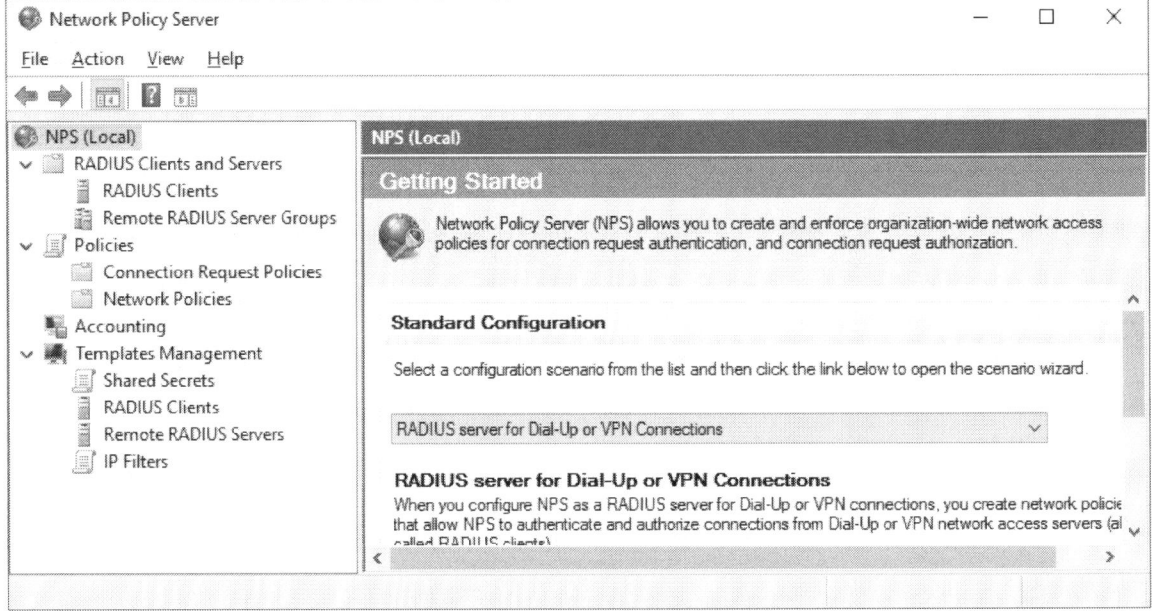

Figure 6.5: NPS Manager Window

Right-click the *NPS (Local)* menu item and select the option to register the NPS server in Active Directory. This gives the RADIUS process the rights to query Active Directory for login credentials.

---

[1] For more information see the Microsoft NPS article at the following URL: https://docs.microsoft.com/en-us/windows-server/networking/technologies/nps/nps-top

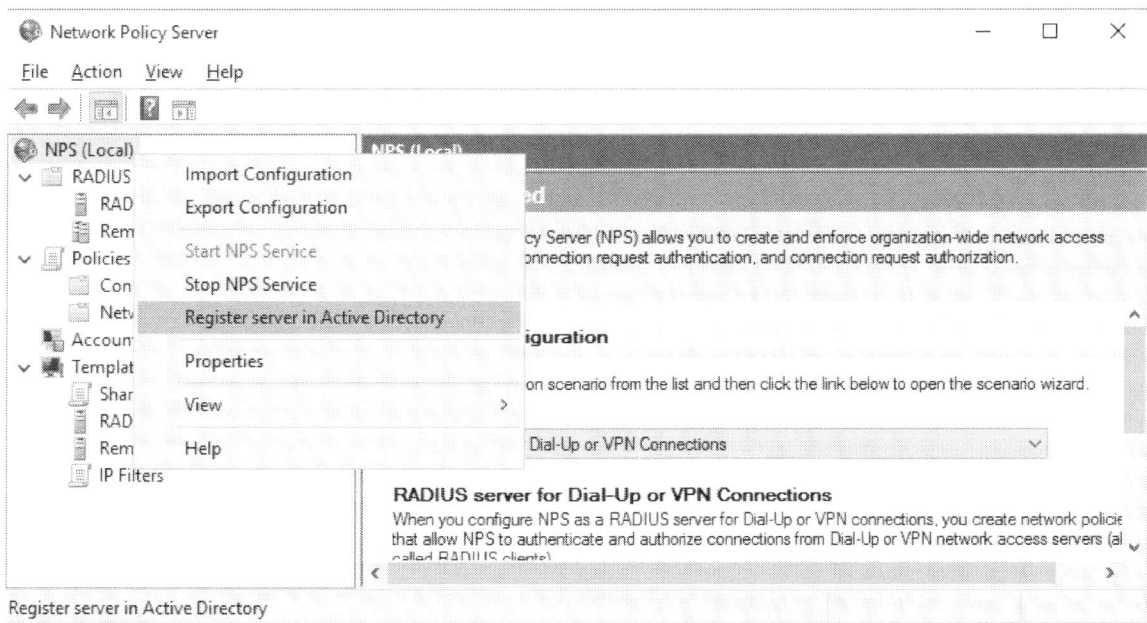

Figure 6.6: Register NPS with Active Directory

Select the option in the pop-up dialog to register the NPS server with Active Directory.

While many RADIUS clients can use encryption to secure authentication traffic that feature isn't included in RouterOS. The MikroTik implementation uses Password Authentication Protocol (PAP) for authentication, and by default PAP is not enabled in the NPS role. Use the following steps to enable PAP for NPS:

1. Expand *Policies* in the left menu

2. Select *Connection Request Policies*

3. Right-click the default *Use Windows authentication for all users* and select *Properties*

4. Select *Authentication Methods* in the left menu

5. Check the box for *Override network policy authentication settings*

6. Check the box for *Unencrypted authentication (PAP, SPAP)*

7. Acknowledge the warning about the insecure protocol[2]

8. Click *OK*

---

[2] While I would normally not advocate using a protocol like PAP, I think the security benefits of consolidating AAA outweigh the risks if networks are segmented and monitored properly.

Grant User Logon Rights

All users who authenticate to the router via RADIUS need authorization in Active Directory. Only network administrators and technicians with a real need should have these rights. The following steps configure Active Directory objects and create a network policy for controlling device access with domain credentials:

1. Configure Active Directory objects:

    (a) Create user groups in ADUC:

    - *MikroTik Admins* for network administrators
    - *MikroTik Analysts* for less-experienced technicians

    The following PowerShell command creates the *MikroTik Admins* group and can be adapted for other groups as well:

    ```
    New-ADGroup -Name "MikroTik Admins" -GroupScope
        Universal -Description "MikroTik administrators
        with full privileges"
    ```

    (b) Add Active Directory users to the groups created above as appropriate

2. Create an NPS policy:

    (a) In the NPS manager expand *Policies* in the left menu

    (b) Right-click *Network Policies* and select *New*

    (c) Give the policy a name and leave the type as *Unspecified*, then click *Next*

3. Specify policy conditions:

    (a) Click the *Add* button a create a condition

    (b) Select *Windows Groups* and click *Add*

    (c) Click *Add Groups*, search for and select the *MikroTik Admins* group created previously, then click *OK* and *Next*

    (d) Verify that *Access Granted* is selected, then click *Next*

    (e) Check the box for *Unencrypted authentication (PAP, SPAP)*, note the warning dialog, then click *Next*

4. Configure policy constraints:

    (a) Enter a value for *Idle Timeout*[3] if required by your organization's security policy

    (b) Enter a value for *Session Timeout* if required by your organization's security policy

    (c) Enter values for *Day and time restrictions* if your organization limits device access to certain days or times

    (d) Click *Next* after the values have been entered

5. Configure vendor-specific RADIUS settings:

    (a) Under *RADIUS Attributes* select *Vendor Specific*, then click *Add*

    (b) Under *Vendor* select *Custom*, then select *Vendor-Specific* and click *Add*

    (c) Click *Add* in the Attribute Information dialog

    (d) Select *Enter vendor code* and use the number *14988*

    (e) Select the *Yes. It conforms* option

    (f) Click *Configure Attribute*

    (g) Enter or select the following:

     - Vendor-assigned attribute number: *3*

     - Attribute format: *String*

     - Attribute value[4]: *full* Use a different group name if you've created custom permissions for specific users.

    (h) Click *OK* three times, then click *Close*

    (i) Click *Next*, then click *Finish*

Add MikroTik RADIUS Clients

Before RouterOS can use the policies and attributes we've already created there must be a configured RADIUS client for each device. Use the following steps in the NPS management console to configure RADIUS clients:

1. Expand *RADIUS Clients and Servers* on the left

2. Right-click *RADIUS Clients* and select *New*

3. Verify the box for *Enable this RADIUS client* is checked

4. Give the client a descriptive name, then enter the IP or DNS name

---

[3] Five or ten minutes seems to be fairly standard across the industry
[4] This is the group name on page 67

5. Enter the case-sensitive shared secret for the RADIUS client (used again on p. 86)

Use the Shared Secrets and RADIUS Clients template functionality in the left menu if you're configuring many MikroTik RADIUS clients. First create the Shared Secret template, then choose it from the drop-down menu while creating the RADIUS client using the previous steps. Ansible or another third-party tool can then be used to update the RADIUS secrets remotely without manual entry on every RouterOS device.

RouterOS Configuration

The MikroTik configuration must match the secret and address configured in Section 6 on page 79. The authentication process on RouterOS checks local credentials first then other AAA sources like RADIUS if configured.

Enable RADIUS for AAA

RouterOS must be configured to use RADIUS for AAA operations before it will begin reaching out to the external server. Use the following command to point RouterOS to RADIUS for AAA first:

```
/user aaa set use-radius=yes accounting=yes
```

> **NOTE**: RouterOS will try to authenticate users with local credentials first if there is a matching username set on the local device. Don't have matching usernames on both the local device and on the FreeRADIUS server.

Using the *"accounting=yes"* option allows us to centralize AAA event logging on the FreeRADIUS or NPS server.

RouterOS RADIUS Client

Use the following commands to point RouterOS at the FreeRADIUS or Windows NPS server on *192.168.88.10* for *login* authentication:

```
/radius
add service=login address=192.168.88.10 secret="abc123!"
```

The same configuration in Winbox is shown in Figure 6.7:

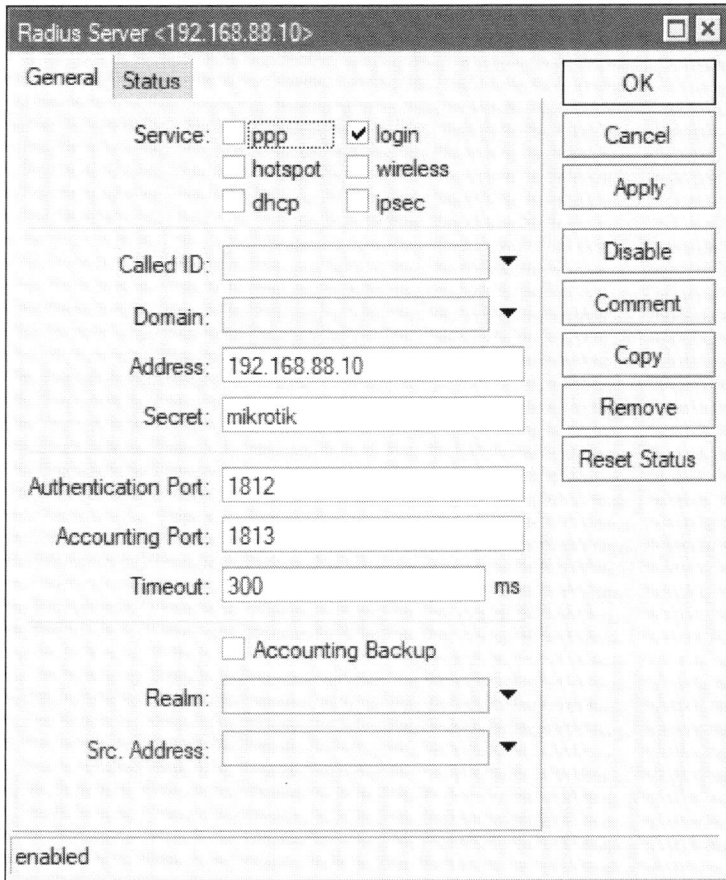

Figure 6.7: RouterOS RADIUS Host

RADIUS Statistics

The RADIUS server statistics are easily available in Winbox or at the console as shown in Figure 6.8:

```
[admin@MikroTik] > /radius monitor 0
         pending: 0
        requests: 18
         accepts: 12
         rejects: 0
         resends: 18
        timeouts: 6
     bad-replies: 0
last-request-rtt: 10ms
[admin@MikroTik] > _
```

Figure 6.8: Terminal RADIUS Status

> **NOTE**: A spike in the *Rejects* counter value could indicate a password guessing attack in-progress.

Timeouts and resends can indicate spotty network connectivity with the AAA server, which was introduced in the lab environment to simulate lost packets for Figure 6.8 on the previous page.

RADIUS Best Practices

Keep in the mind these best practices for centralized RADIUS authentication:

- Make regular backups of the following FreeRADIUS files:

    1. */etc/freeradius/3.0/users*
    2. */etc/freeradius/3.0/clients.conf*
    3. */etc/freeradius/3.0/radiusd.conf*

- Utilize replication and HA features if running virtual servers
- If using NPS on Microsoft Windows Server consider running the role as part of a Windows Failover Cluster
- Build redundant network paths between network clients and RADIUS servers
- Have an "emergency" local user on all devices in case of catastrophic RADIUS infrastructure failure
- Regularly audit configured users in RADIUS or Active Directory and prune them as necessary

Chapter 7

Wireless

With wireless access being essential in modern networks and so many RouterBoard models coming with built-in wireless it's important to secure wireless access. We can leverage encryption, strong keys, access lists, and wireless network segmentation to secure wireless networks from outside and inside attackers.

Encryption

RouterOS supports both WPA and WPA2 encryption, and the legacy (and very unsecure) WEP standard. If at all possible WPA2 of some type should be used to encrypt network traffic, and all modern wireless clients support it. If for whatever reason WEP or WPA must still be used it should have a very robust key set and changed periodically.

WPA2-PSK

Wi-Fi (Wi-Fi) Protected Access 2 (WPA2)-Pre-Shared Key (PSK) uses a PSK to secure communications between clients and Access Points (APs). Using a PSK is convenient and doesn't require any enterprise infrastructure on the back-end to process authentication. Unfortunately, a change to the PSK requires that the new key be sent to all clients. If the PSK is leaked to an untrusted party a wireless network may be compromised. An employee that leaves an organization with the PSK unchanged could access a company network from the parking lot if the signal is good enough. The robustness of protection provided by WPA2-PSK is also directly tied to the strength of the PSK. If the PSK is easily guessable (e.g. Password, P@ssw0rd, 123456789, qwerty, etc.) or written somewhere in plain sight it will be ineffective.

WPA2-Enterprise

WPA2-Enterprise uses Extensible Authentication Protocol (EAP) or Protected EAP (PEAP) to authenticate clients over the network before allowing them to fully connect. The 802.1X standard enables authentication via an infrastructure server running FreeRADIUS, Microsoft Active Directory with NPS, and others. This configuration allows for the following:

1. Easier, centralized credential updates
2. Quick disabling of network access
3. Enforcement of password policies:
    - Length
    - Complexity
    - Age and History
4. Accounting of failed and successful login attempts

For large networks with many roaming wireless clients this kind of Network Access Control (NAC) is essential. The same steps already completed when configuring RADIUS for local authentication can be used to configure 802.1X for wireless access. Unfortunately I haven't been able to develop a consistent set of WPA2-Enterprise implementation steps for RouterOS. Issues with different versions of RouterOS and the unique "quirks" of FreeRADIUS and Windows Server NPS have caused people to struggle for years while configuring secure wireless access. Hopefully in the future WPA2-Enterprise implementation for MikroTik networks will become more straightforward for enterprise network operators.

WPS

Wi-Fi Protected Setup (WPS) makes wireless configuration easy for home users. This feature simplifies the process of adding additional devices to an existing network, but a secure network must already be available to join. While WPS does offer convenience it's also easily exploited by attackers when not implemented correctly. Many network administrators leave the feature turned off or only use it when other solutions aren't available for this reason.

Security Profiles

The Security Profile brings together encryption, PSKs, Remote Authentication Dial-In User Service (RADIUS), and EAP settings. Each reusable profile can then be assigned to physical or virtual wireless interfaces to control network access. Security Profiles are local to each RouterOS device, so changes to settings on one AP won't affect another. An example of a new wireless security profile being created with a WPA2 PSK is shown in Figure 7.1.

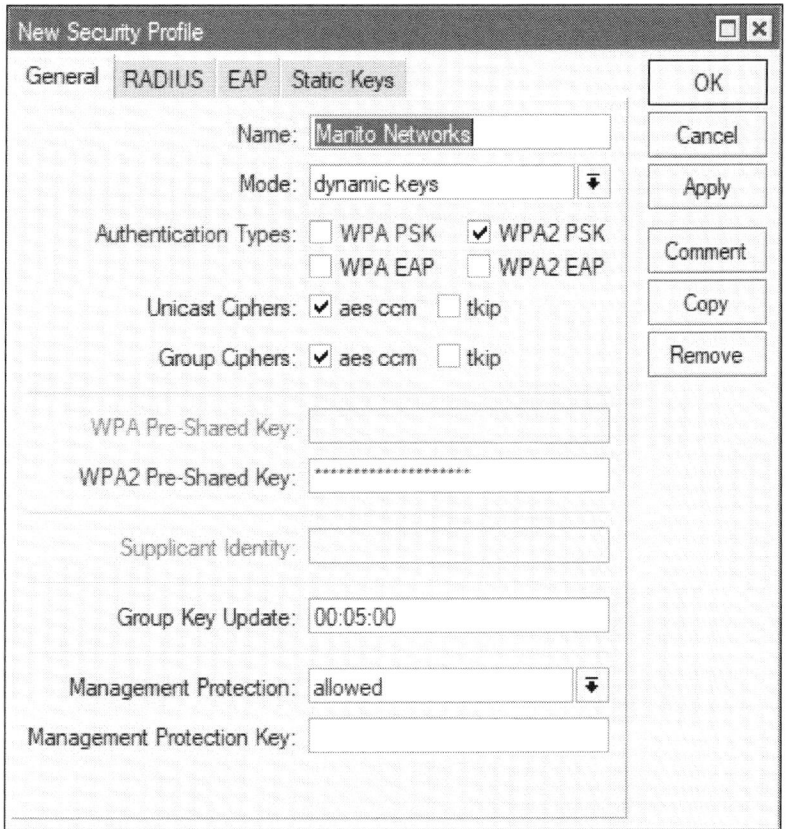

Figure 7.1: New Wireless Security Profile

While both Temporal Key Integrity Protocol (TKIP) and AES encryption are available, AES is the most secure. TKIP may be required for very legacy devices but otherwise shouldn't be used in modern networks. Once a wireless security profile has been created it can be applied directly to a wireless network interface along with an Service Set Identifier (SSID) as shown in Figure 7.2 on the next page.

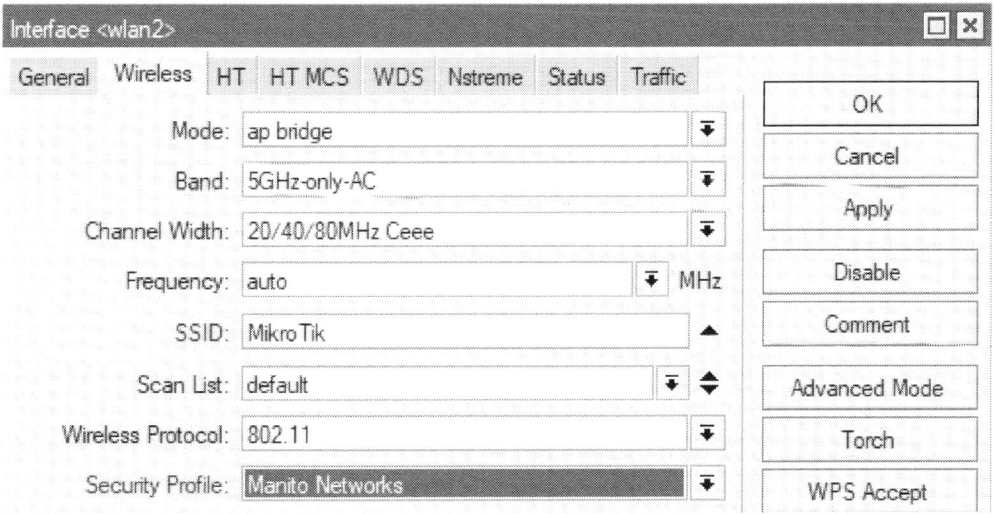

Figure 7.2: Selecting a Wireless Security Profile

WPS Mode

The following modes of adding devices to a network are available in RouterOS or typical of other platforms:

- Push Button
- Virtual Push Button
- PIN (not supported in RouterOS)

The WPS Personal Identification Number (PIN) method isn't available in RouterOS for security reasons. Some vendors place a sticker on their wireless units with the PIN which creates a security issue. Other router platforms have been found with hard-coded WPS PINs, which provide little or no security. Not all RouterBoard models have a physical WPS button, but all RouterOS versions support the virtual button.

WPS is disabled by default on some units[1] but it's simple to enable the physical button (if available) for an interface with the following command:

```
/interface wireless
set wlan1 wps-mode=push-button
```

To only use the *WPS Accept* button in Winbox instead use the "*wps-mode=push-button-virtual-only*" option. This allows network administrators some amount of control along with the convenience of WPS.

Access Lists

Using an Access List can help administrators limit devices on wireless networks to those that need it and meet security requirements, including the following:

- Updated software
- PIN code or password set
- Device encryption

Devices are entered by MAC address and each can be assigned a unique wireless encryption key. The benefit of these lists is having more granular control over devices that can access the network, even including the days and times that access is allowed. The following commands create an Access List entry for an imaginary Android device with the MAC address *AA:BB:CC:DD:EE:FF*:

```
/interface wireless access-list
add mac-address=AA:BB:CC:DD:EE:FF interface=all private-pre-
    shared-key="my-great-key!" comment="Tyler Hart Android"
```

---

[1] https://wiki.mikrotik.com/wiki/Manual:Interface/Wireless

Figure 7.3 on the next page shows an existing device in the Access List and a new device being created. The device has a unique key assigned and is allowed to access the wireless network on weekdays.

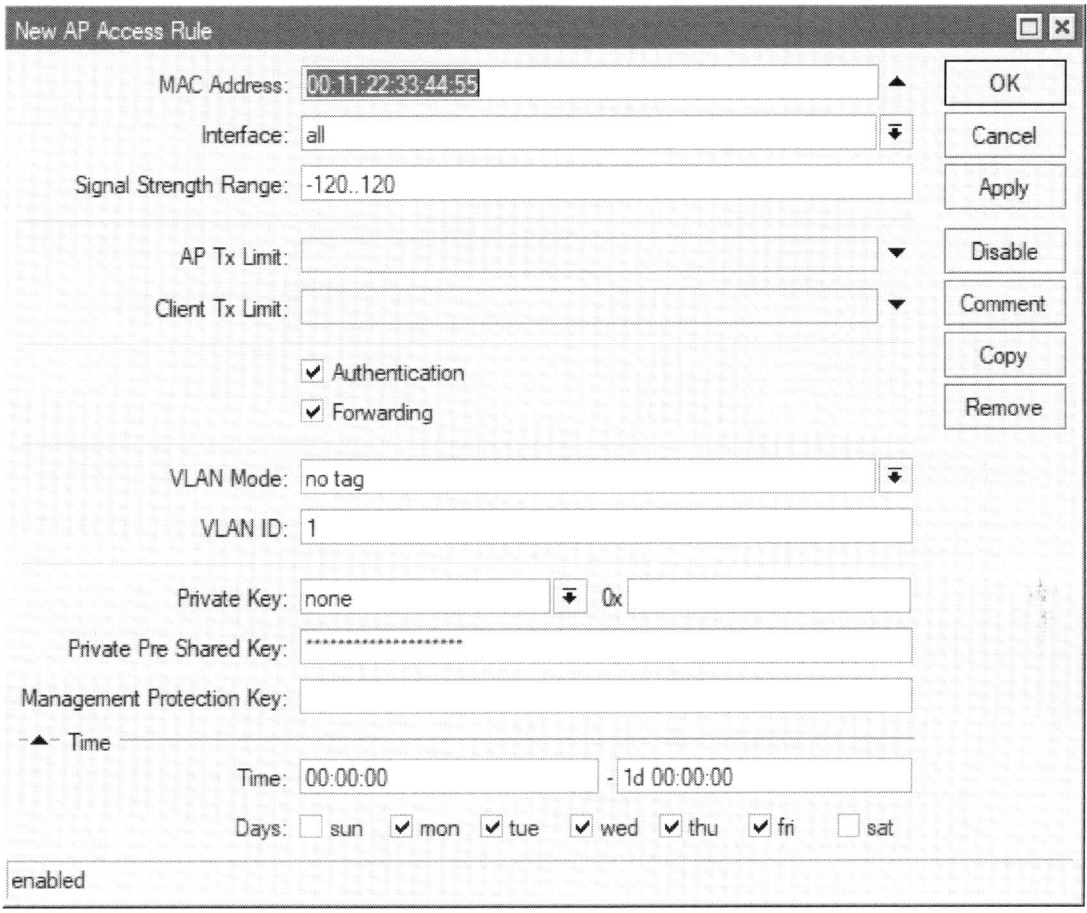

Figure 7.3: Wireless Access List

Use Access Lists to ensure only authorized devices can use wireless networks and audit them regularly to remove old entries of phased-out devices. Should one user's wireless key be improperly shared or compromised it can be updated without disturbing everyone else's wireless access.

> **NOTE**: Add a comment to each device on the Access List with the owner's name so you know who to contact immediately if there is suspicious network activity around the device.

Client Isolation

Many vendors implement a client isolation feature that either allows or blocks other hosts on the same wireless network from communicating. In RouterOS there is no option explicitly named "Client Isolation" or "Wireless Isolation" but there is the "*Default Forward*" option. The checkbox that turns this feature on and off can be seen in the lower middle area of Figure 7.2 on page 92. This option is enabled on all wireless networks by default and hosts are able to communicate with one another and the AP. By unchecking the box it's possible to isolate the hosts from one another, which is great for guest wireless or hospitality networks.

> **NOTE**: In wireless networks with streaming media devices unchecking this box will most likely break that functionality because hosts can't communicate via the AP, despite being on the same wireless network.

Chapter 8

Best Practices

This chapter covers some industry-standard best practices. These are widely considered to be tasks that prudent network operators and system administrators perform to secure networks and keep them running over the long-term.

Run Current Stable Software

Devices on production networks should run the latest stable software available for their platform. This ensures that vendor patches for security issues are applied to support the *confidentiality* and *integrity* of your systems. The latest stable release may also include improvements in platform performance and stability which can have an impact on the *availability* of your networks.

Set Software Package Channel

A few package channels exist and you can select which branch you'd like. The **current** branch is always recommended because it's the latest stable release appropriate for production networks:

```
/system package update set channel=current
```

Check for Updates

With the channel selected run the update check:

```
/system package update check-for-updates
```

Download Updates

If a new version is available download it:

```
/system package update download
```

Reboot

New package files being detected in the file system will trigger the install when the device reboots. **This will incur about 1-2 minutes of downtime depending on the platform.** Kick off the installation by rebooting the router:

```
/system reboot
```

Run Current Firmware

Regularly checking for firmware updates ensures that devices run the latest and most secure bootloader. First check for updates using the "*/system routerboard print*" command shown in Figure 8.1.

```
[admin@MikroTik] > /system routerboard print
routerboard: yes
model: RouterBOARD 952Ui-5ac2nD
serial-number: 6CBA06ED497F
firmware-type: qca9531L
factory-firmware: 3.29
current-firmware: 3.39
upgrade-firmware: 3.39
[admin@MikroTik] > _
```

Figure 8.1: RouterBoard Version

This router has the latest firmware installed and no new version is available. The factory firmware version cannot be upgraded, and it's the bootloader that a hard-reset using the physical button would use. To upgrade a router or other device if a new firmware version is available use the following command:

```
/system routerboard upgrade
```

Running the upgrade command will not reboot the router without further confirmation but the upgrade won't complete until a reboot occurs.

Reverse Path Filtering (Forwarding)

Best practices[1] dictate using some kind of ingress filtering like Reverse Path Filtering (RPF), also known as Reverse Path Forwarding. This feature drops packet traffic that appears to be spoofed, e.g. packets from LAN subnets heading outbound but with a different source IP address than the local network's. This is very common when a workstation has been infected with a virus and co-opted into a botnet. Use the following to implement Reverse Path Filtering (RPF):

```
/ip settings set rp-filter=strict
```

> **NOTE**: The Reverse Path Filter feature can cause issues if a router is multi-homed. MikroTik's implementation of this feature doesn't allow Reverse Path Filtering to be enabled on specific interfaces. As of this writing it can only be enabled or disabled for the entire device.

Login Banner

We should also set a login banner that is displayed when someone logs (or attempts to log) into the router. This is required by a number of compliance standards, and is also defined in a STIG. For organizations like the US DoD this type of banner is required per Infrastructure Router STIG Finding V-3013:

> "Network devices must display the... approved logon banner warning."

Depending on the country and jurisdiction you're in this banner statement may or may not be legally relevant, but it certainly doesn't hurt to have a banner displayed on login. First, set the banner to be displayed at login:

```
/system note set show-at-login=yes
```

Then set the contents of the banner message. This should be something that clearly states that access to the router is for authorized administrators only and that access is monitored. Consult with a legal professional in your area for the appropriate verbiage

```
/system note set note="Authorized administrators only. Access
    to this device is monitored."
```

---

[1] http://www.bcp38.info/index.php/Main_Page

Now when an administrator (or anyone else) logs into the router remotely via SSH or Telnet this banner will appear. It will also appear when a terminal is opened in Winbox. An example of the banner that was set previously is shown in Figure 8.2:

```
Authorized administrators only. Access to this device is
    monitored.

[admin@MikroTik] > _
```

Figure 8.2: Displaying Login Banner

NTP Clock Synchronization

We should also set the router to synchronize its clock with an NTP server, so the router and other infrastructure devices remain coordinated with an accurate clock. When a router's clock isn't correct any log analysis or log correlation becomes very difficult because the timestamps can't be trusted. Set the NTP client up to use the NTP.org pool project and Google's NTP servers:

```
/system ntp client
set enabled=yes server-dns-names=0.pool.ntp.org,1.pool.ntp.
    org,2.pool.ntp.org,3.pool.ntp.org,time.google.com
```

Setting multiple NTP servers satisfies Infrastructure Router STIG Finding V-23747:

> "Network devices must use at least two NTP servers to synchronize time."

Many organizations set their infrastructure device time zones to UTC so that all timestamps match across devices and don't have to be adjusted for local time when doing log analysis. Using UTC also helps when networks span multiple geographies that handle Daylight Savings Time differently.

Dude Syslog Event Logging

Syslog is one of the most widely supported event reporting mechanisms. It is implemented across almost all manufacturers and router software distributions. Using Syslog to report events happening on routers, switches, and servers is typical and centrally monitoring events is important. Most organizations don't report every single event because that would create an unmanageable mess of logs. Instead administrators focus on hardware events, authentication issues, interface up / down events, and network adjacency changes.

RouterOS Syslog Configuration

First create a Syslog action with the following command that points to a Syslog server like The Dude at 192.168.88.10:

```
/system logging action
add bsd-syslog=yes name=Syslog remote=192.168.88.10 target=
    remote
```

With the action created it can be used for specific types of events like critical-level hardware changes and account actions:

```
/system logging
add topics=critical,error,account action=Syslog disabled=no
```

Once Syslog events are shipped to a central server it's possible to trigger email or text message alerts with the right third-party software. The next section enables the service server-side and configures alerts.

Dude Server Syslog Settings

The Dude server must have the Syslog service enabled before messages from reporting devices will be logged and displayed. The *Settings* button on the left in the Dude client opens a series of tabs as shown in Figure 8.3:

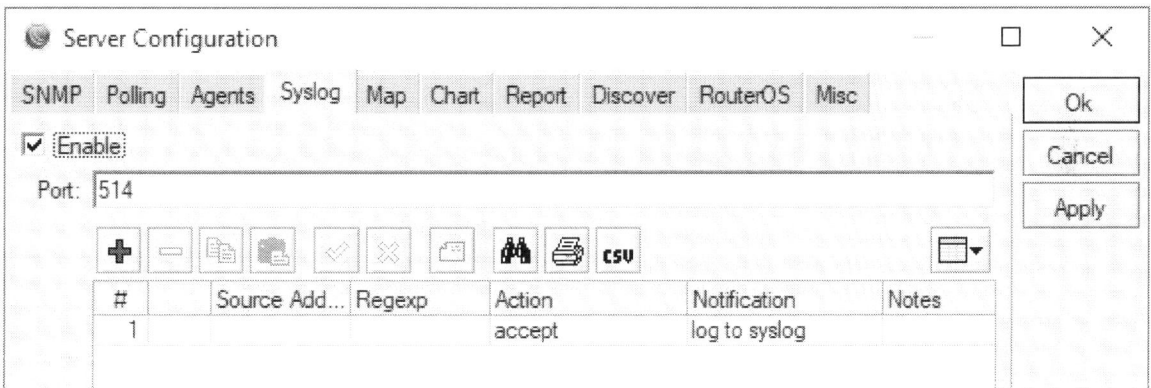

Figure 8.3: Dude Syslog Settings

First verify that the *Enable* box is checked on the Syslog tab. Port 514 is the typical port number and won't need to be changed if you're only using the configuration commands in this book. This is all the configuration necessary to begin logging event data from RouterOS devices. Double-clicking *Log* in the Dude client's left menu pane opens the running log of events. Figure 8.4 on the next page shows typical entries like "...*user tyler logged in*..." and "...*user tyler logged out*...".

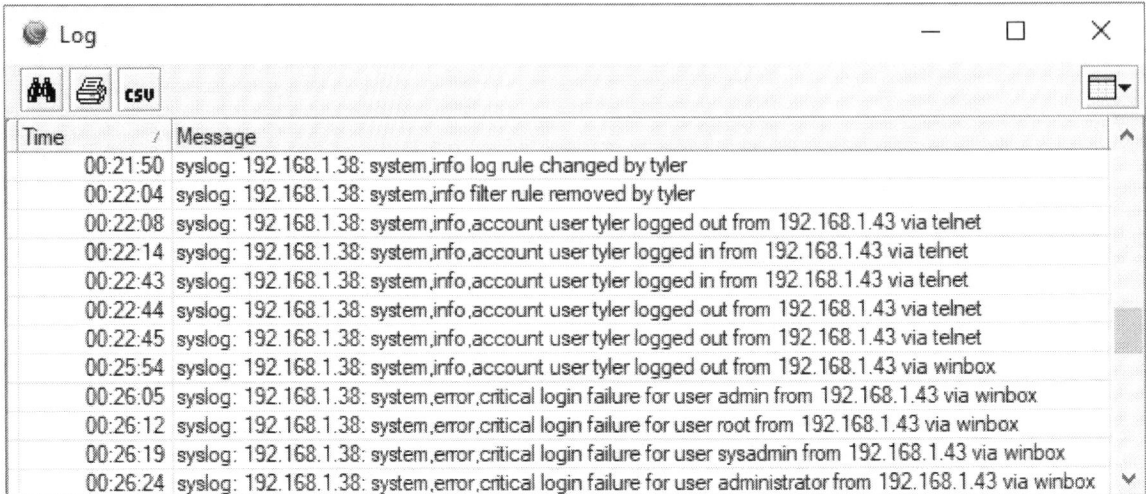

Figure 8.4: Dude Syslog Events

At the same time Figure 8.4 also shows suspicious failed login attempts for *root*, *administrator*, and *sysadmin* users. These entries can indicate an attacker looking for soft targets with typical factory-default settings still in-place.

Dude SNMP Monitoring

The SNMP protocol will provide us with a wealth of device performance information once we configure a profile on the Dude server. On page 34 we created an SNMP community and here is where it's put to work. Figure 8.5 shows the default SNMP profiles that come pre-configured on the Dude server under the far-left *Settings* menu in the *SNMP tab*:

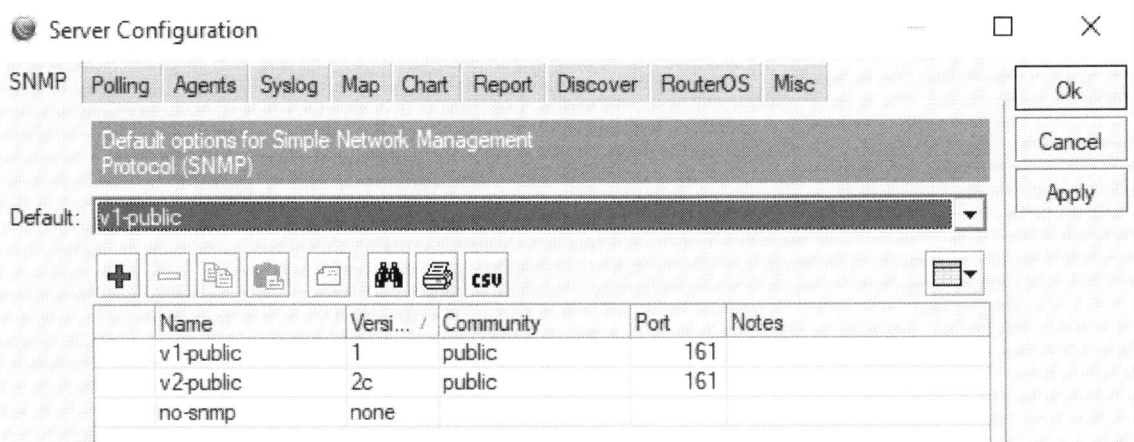

Figure 8.5: Dude Default SNMP Profiles

These would work fine for us with a device fresh out-of-the-box but we disabled the default *public* community on page 34. Click the button to add a new profile and fill in your SNMP community information as shown in Figure 8.6 on the following page:

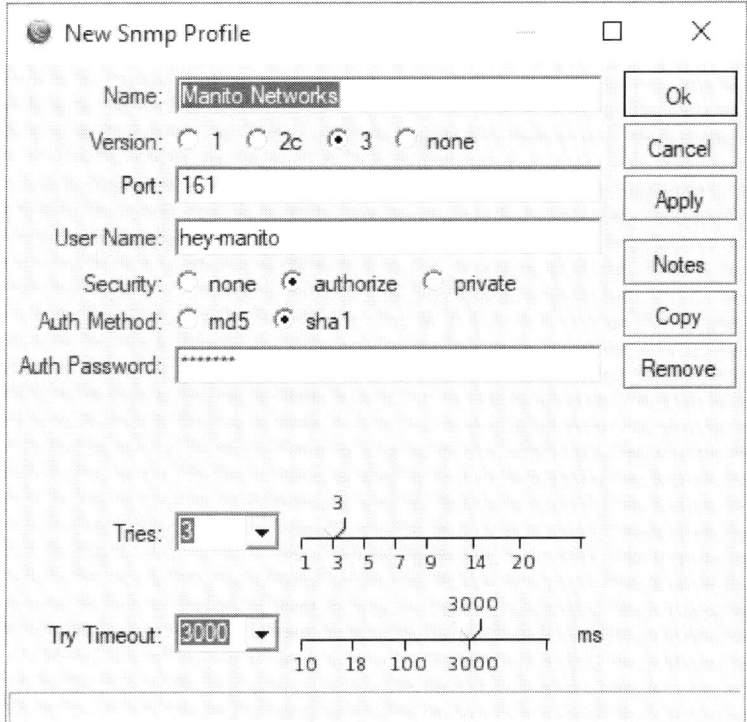

Figure 8.6: Dude New SNMP Profile

Since Dude is running on RouterOS we can also do the same configuration in Winbox as shown in Figure 8.7 on the next page:

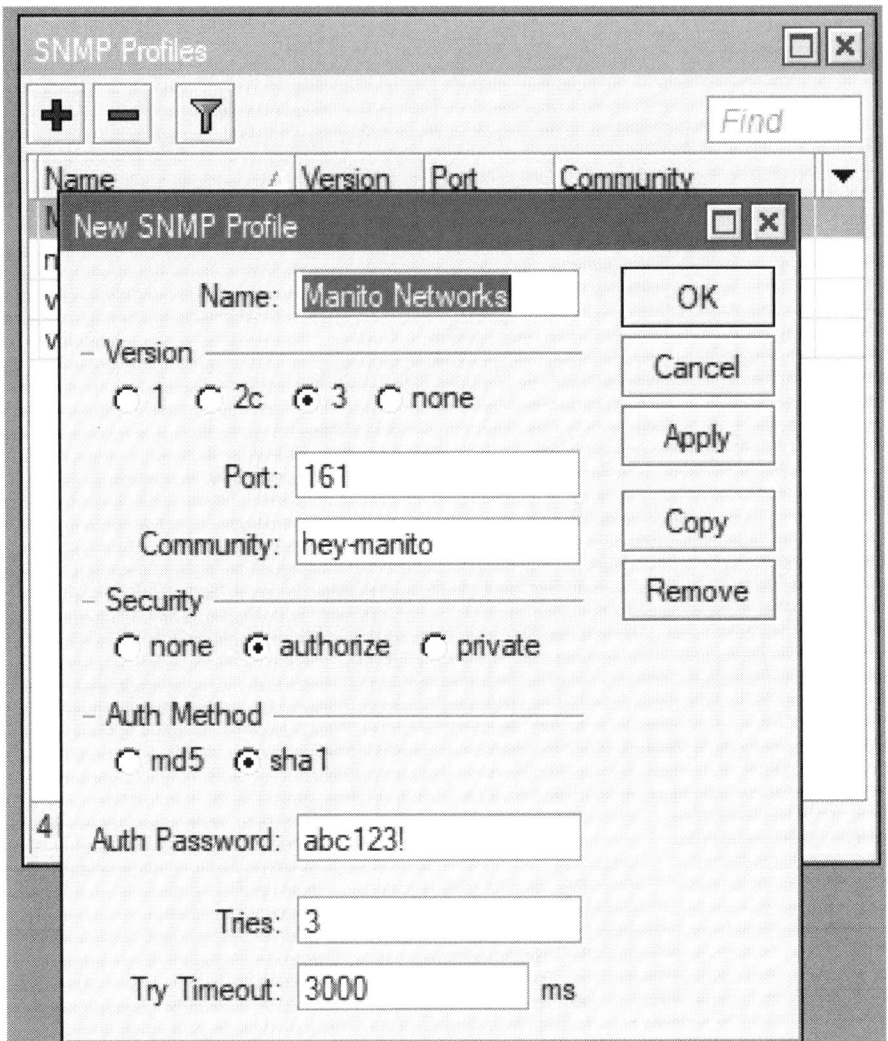

Figure 8.7: Dude SNMP Profile in Winbox

While SNMP is usually a polling protocol where nothing is exchanged unless the collector reaches out we can have RouterOS send SNMP Traps. These special pieces of information are normally sent only when something interesting happens on a device. RouterOS has limited functionality for sending traps but it can alert on interface-related events. When discussing physical security on page 1 it was mentioned that an attacker unplugging an interface should trigger an alert. These steps are where we implement that alerting and the single command on RouterOS would make a good addition to your default configuration templates.

The following RouterOS command configures SNMP traps to be sent when *ether1* through *ether3* experience a change:

```
/snmp
set trap-target=192.168.88.10 trap-community=hey-manito trap-
  version=3 trap-generators=interfaces trap-interfaces=
  ether1,ether2,ether3
```

Figure 8.8 shows the configuration applied in Winbox:

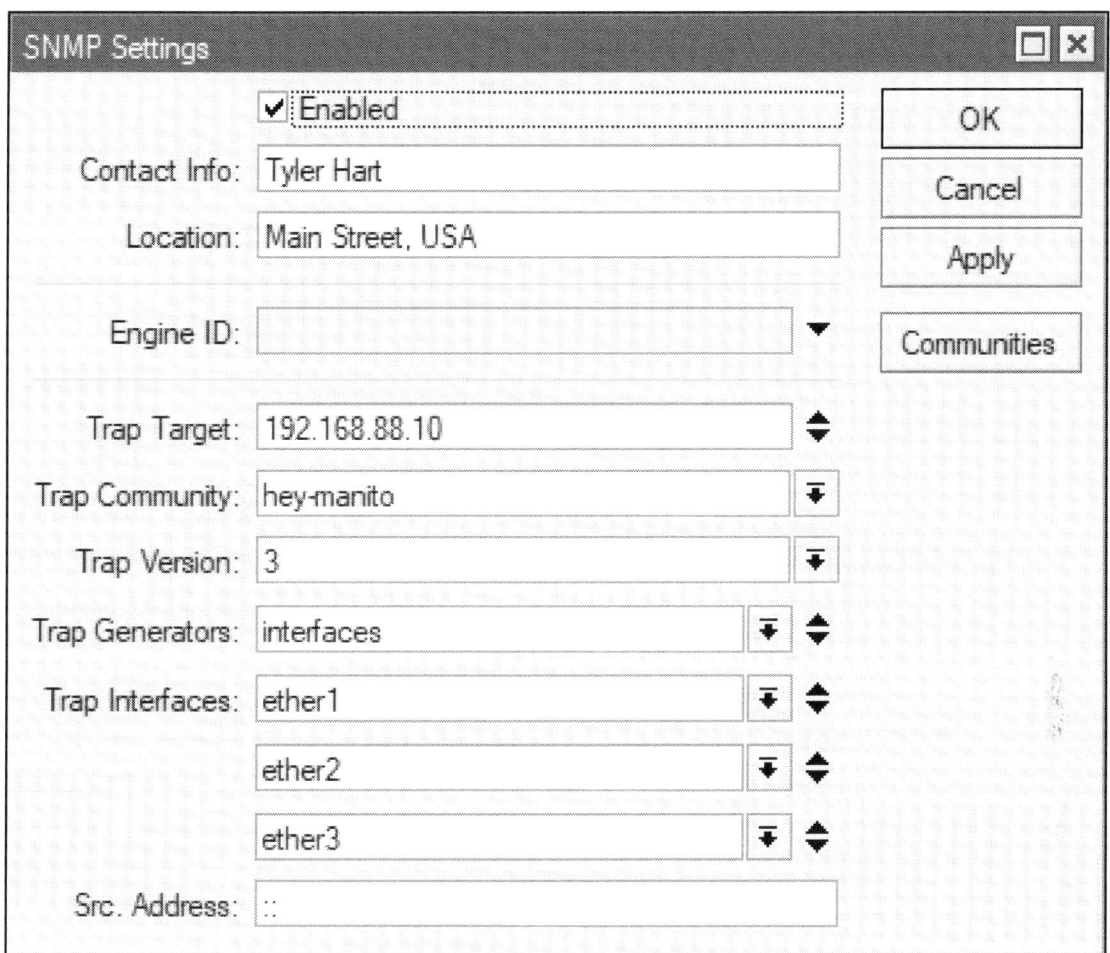

Figure 8.8: Winbox SNMP Trap Configuration

SMB Shares

RouterOS has the capability of sharing files and folders over the network. This can make it very easy to move files on and off the device but it can also expose confidential information. SMB sharing is turned off but the other settings aren't very secure if it were enabled on the device. Figure 8.9 shows the default SMB sharing configuration:

```
[admin@MikroTik] > /ip smb print
enabled: no
domain: MSHOME
comment: MikrotikSMB
allow-guests: yes
interfaces: all
[admin@MikroTik] > _
```

Figure 8.9: Default SMB Settings

While it is disabled by default it only takes one command to turn it on. With the other default settings in place guest access would be allowed and it would be listening for connections on all interfaces. We should do the following things to secure SMB:

- Use a non-standard SMB domain
- Forbid guest access
- Disable the service

Complete the tasks above with the following commands:

```
/ip smb
set enabled=no allow-guests=no domain=blahblahblah
```

Turning guest access off now ensures that if the service get turns back on guest access won't be allowed unless someone takes that additional step. In RouterOS as of this writing the built-in guest account can't be removed or disabled as shown in Figure 8.10 on the following page:

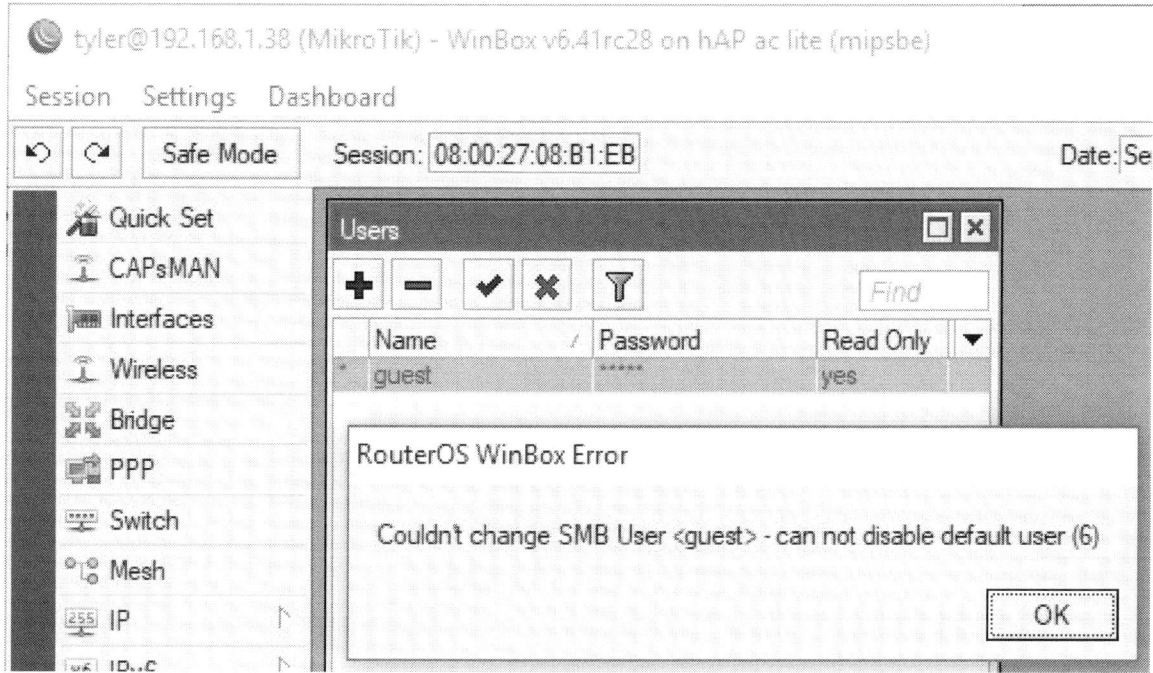

Figure 8.10: SMB Guest User

However, we can change the default account with the following command so password-guessing attacks won't be successful:

```
/ip smb users
set [find name=guest] name=blah password=abc123! read-only=
   yes
```

Backups

Having viable backups and creating regular backup copies is an important part of security. If a device is stolen or fails catastrophically you must be able to restore services quickly. Having viable backups archived and available for restore directly affects the *availability* of your networks.

Device Backup

To create a binary device backup for restore directly to the same device use the following:

```
/system backup save name=bin_backup password=abc123!
```

This is an encrypted, password protected binary backup that can be applied to the same device it was created on.

Configuration Backup

If you need to export the human-readable configuration to apply to another device or to use as a template perform the following:

```
/export file=config_backup
```

Make backups as configurations are changed, and on a regular basis during normal operations. Secure backup configurations in a safe place with access limited to those who need it. Keeping a configuration backup both on-site and off-site can help mitigate the threat of fire or other natural disaster that causes the loss of an entire location.

Wiping Devices

MikroTik devices are typically very robust and can run for years without failure. When devices leave production and get repurposed as bench-testing units or are transferred to another organization they should be wiped first. This ensures that no one has access to user credentials, wireless keys, and other sensitive information. The command in Figure 8.11 completely resets a device to factory defaults:

```
[admin@MikroTik] > /system reset-configuration keep-users=no
    skip-backup=yes
Dangerous! Reset anyway? [y/N]:
y
system configuration will be reset
```

Figure 8.11: Resetting Device Configuration

The configuration reset can also be done via Winbox as shown in Figure 8.12:

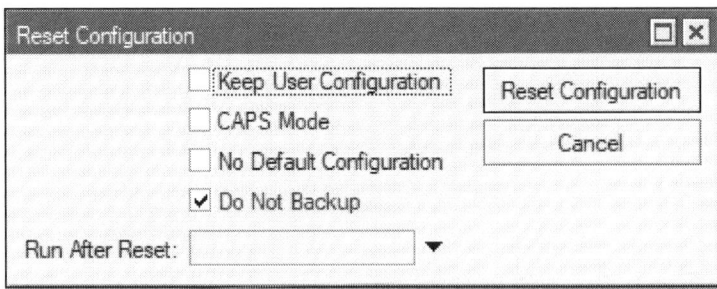

Figure 8.12: Winbox Reset Configuration

The "/system reset-configuration..." command does not delete files from the onboard storage so it's important to remove those manually. The following commands remove important files that can include sensitive information:

```
/file remove [find name~".rsc"]
/file remove [find name~".backup"]
/file remove [find name~".txt"]
```

These commands could be copied and pasted into an *.rsc* file and uploaded to the device. Then that file could be run using the *"run-after-reset"* command option if you're wiping devices in bulk.

Summary

Network security isn't something you do once and forget - it's part of your organization's technology culture. The best organizations I've worked and consulted with are those that continually evaluate their own networks and operational practices. When self-evaluation is part of your regular operations it's easy to pass network audits and stay secure over the long-term. Remember the CIA triad and how it affects your network operations. Maintaining the confidentiality, integrity, and availability of your networks is at the core of what we're doing. By diving into firewall rules, port scans, performance statistics, and more you can also begin to ask really interesting questions about your own infrastructure.

Thank you for taking the time to read this book and good luck in securing, growing, and maintaining your networks.

Made in the USA
Monee, IL
24 August 2020